Gillian Spraggs was b
PhD from the Univer
seventeenth-century literature and has published several critical essays, including one on Sappho, and another on the poetry of Sylvia Townsend Warner and Valentine Ackland. She has also published numerous reviews and articles, a short story and several poems. She spends most of her time reading, and much of the rest hunting through second-hand bookshops. She lives in Leicestershire, in a house with far too many books, and is working on a volume of translations of poems by Renée Vivien.

To Sue,
with thanks for your
help & much love,
Gill

love shook my senses

Lesbian Love Poems

GILLIAN SPRAGGS, EDITOR

First published by The Women's Press Ltd, 1998
A member of the Namara Group
34 Great Sutton Street, London EC1V 0DX

British Library Cataloguing-in-Publication Data
A catalogue record for this book is available from the British Library.

ISBN 0 7043 4581 1

Typeset in Sabon by FSH Ltd, London
Printed and bound in Great Britain by Cox & Wyman Ltd, Reading, Berkshire

for Mog

CONTENTS

'NOTHING IS SWEETER THAN LOVE'

'I DID NOT LIVE UNTIL THIS TIME'

'Love, love, the dogs are after me'

ACKNOWLEDGEMENTS

I am conscious of owing many debts. Marion Shaw's advice on how to proceed was invaluable from the outset. Emma Donoghue also shared with me a great deal of advice and information, based on her own recent experiences as an anthologist. Without her help, this anthology would have been much more arduous to compile.

I owe a special debt to Alison Hennegan: for her sound advice on many matters, for sharing her extensive scholarly knowledge of lesbian writing, for allowing me to use her superb collection of books and for her hospitality while I was staying in Cambridge.

I am extremely grateful to Claire Wintram for her advice on the translations from the French of Renée Vivien. She is not, of course, responsible for any questionable decisions I may have made.

Christina Dunhill put me in touch with several of the poets whose work is included in this anthology. Eve Grainger put me up while I was staying in London. Francis Bowdery explained the allusions to Beethoven's Third Symphony in Amy Levy's poem 'Sinfonia Eroica'. Emma Donoghue explained the reference to Durdans in Michael Field's poem 'Second Thoughts'.

Many people have allowed me to use their copies of hard-to-come-by poetry volumes. I am particularly grateful to Jane Anger, Helen Columbine and Shirley Williamson, Jan Crew, Joyce Freya, Caroline Gonda, Margaret Gregory, Simon Miles, Jill Parker, Sarah Roelofs, Jan Sellers, Jayne Shakespeare, Deborah Tyler-Bennett and Diana Wallace.

I should like to thank Barbara Burford, Sally Cline, Diana

Collecott, Meg Davis, Jane Dowson, Claire Harman, Diana Lachatanere of the Schomburg Center for Research in Black Culture, Wendy Mulford, Angela Pitt, Sandi Russell, Sue Sanders, Dorothea Smartt and Chris White, all of whom took the time to answer my enquiries on various points.

Many people, including many already mentioned, have made recommendations of particular poems or poets. I am very grateful to them all.

I greatly appreciate the support and encouragement I have received throughout this project from the members of the Feminist Research Group of Loughborough University English Department. I am particularly grateful to Diana Wallace for commenting on the Preface.

I should like to thank the staffs of the British Library, Cambridge University Library, Leicester University Library, the Pilkington Library of Loughborough University, the library of the Taylorian Institute, Oxford, and especially that unrivalled resource, the Poetry Library in the South Bank Centre, London.

I am grateful to The Women's Press, and Helen Windrath in particular, for inviting me to undertake this project, and for seeing it through to completion.

I should like to thank Mog Singer, who has listened patiently (well, mostly) to a lot of rambling talk, and has read and given her opinion on a large number of poems.

And above all, I should like to express my gratitude to the poets, living and dead.

PREFACE

Love shook my senses
like a wind rushing down upon the oaks of the mountain.

I was sixteen when I first read this fragment of a lost love poem, composed by Sappho more than two and a half millennia ago. The image shook me with immediate recognition. Love – *eros* – sexual passion: that compelling force that comes, apparently, from out of the blue and shakes us to our roots – at that time I was just beginning to know its power.

Traditionally, when passion, or grief, or intense joy disturb the settled patterns of our lives, we turn to poetry – our own, or other people's. We look for words to give a voice to what cries out, unvoiced, within us. With words, we rebuild our disrupted sense of who we are to accommodate a new understanding. Sometimes, if it is passion that has taken hold of us, we feel impelled to construct the beloved in words. It is a way of making love – of taking possession, and also of paying due tribute.

For those of us who are lesbians, this engagement with language has been particularly tricky to negotiate. For us, the disruptive impact of sexual passion is likely to be fiercer, separating us out from family and friends, alienating us from whole areas of cultural tradition. There are old prohibitions on our speech, weaker now than they once were but not yet dissolved. Certain words continue to be sites of conflict, weighted with contempt or embarrassment, hardly to be claimed in public without a measure of defiance. For just these reasons, finding language that voices what we feel and know may be even more crucial to nourishing our sense of who we are than it is for many others. And our survival may depend upon our assembling, more or less deliberately, a tradition of our own out of what we can find available.

And so we have struggled to piece together fragments, of a poem or a life; or we have learned to interpret painstakingly from ambiguities, strategic silences, wilful obscurities, hints. We have learned to look beyond a poet's adoption of a male persona; to disregard the hectoring of biographers and critics who instruct us to 'read heterosexual' against our own perceptions. And we have relished our encounters with the uncompromisingly lesbian text that floats up luminously from the page.

This work is much easier now than it used to be. Over the last twenty-five years or so, the labours of lesbian and feminist historians, biographers, literary scholars and anthologists have made available texts and biographical knowledge that used to be esoteric or simply inaccessible. And of course, during the same time, a great many original poems, novels, memoirs and short stories have come off the presses. Many of the poets represented in this anthology first began publishing during this period. Others, who had already made reputations for themselves, found a new focus and readership within the feminist movement.

Yet among the poets of previous generations there are several important figures whose writings, wholly or in part, remain very hard to lay hands on. The bulk of the poetry of Michael Field (Katharine Bradley and Edith Cooper) is available only on the shelves of major libraries. It is even harder to track down the work of Renée Vivien (Pauline Tarn), an Englishwoman who rejected her nationality and wrote her poems in French. The extraordinary joint volume published by Sylvia Townsend Warner and Valentine Ackland in 1934, *Whether a Dove or Seagull*, has never been reprinted. Most of the contents are love poems; Sylvia's poems to Valentine and Valentine's to Sylvia. Permission to include poems from *Whether a Dove or Seagull* in this anthology has been refused by the literary executor, who also refused permission to reprint some of Valentine Ackland's later love poems. This is a strange and saddening fate for two poets whose openness about their commitment to each other was remarkable in their generation.

What do we find in lesbian love poetry, apart, that is, from the age-old dangerous secret: that one woman can love another with a bodily passion? We find what we might expect to find in love poems: desire, tenderness, sensuousness, delight; and the awareness of mortality, and the anguish of separation and loss. There are rather a lot of love poems between women that are about separation. It is a recurrent theme in Sappho, in Katherine Philips, in other poets who are less well known. It is not hard to see where this comes from. So few women in past societies had more than a very limited control over the circumstances of their lives. Other themes begin to be clearly traceable from the start of the twentieth century: a sense of breaking rules and of taking risks; defiance; a wry awareness of the gap between the private self and the self that is visible to others. Recurrent also, and this is not surprising, is a sense of the beloved as the only safe refuge in a menacing world.

It is sometimes argued that the best love poetry is that which in some sense most inclines towards the universal. I am not persuaded that this is true. I believe that poetry of all kinds is at its finest when it is rooted in the particular. What we respond to in a lover is not, in the end, what she shares with other women, but what is special to her – a look, a gesture, a tone of voice. These are what catch at the heart. The best love poetry wrestles with the problem of communicating the specificity of our experience; and what we most respond to in an individual poem are the qualities that mark it out.

In her poem '7301' U. A. Fanthorpe writes of twenty years of 'learning to read' the woman she loves, 'to master the code'. It is possible to have a relationship with a poem, or with the corpus of a poet's work, that is as compelling and crucial as the relationship with a lover: a connection that keeps on drawing us back, that keeps us attentive, determined 'to master the code'.

Gillian Spraggs

'Love shook my senses'

'Love shook my senses'

Love shook my senses
like a wind rushing down upon the oaks of the mountain.

Sappho

'He seems to me the peer of gods'

He seems to me the peer of gods, that man
who sits and faces you,
close by you hearing
your sweet voice speaking,

and your sexy laugh, which just this moment makes
the heart quake in my breast: for every time
I briefly glance towards you, then I lose
all power of further speech.

My tongue is smashed; at once a film of fire
runs underneath my skin; no image shapes
before my eyes;
my ears are whining like a whirling top;

cold sweat pours down me, and in every part
shuddering grips me;
I am paler than summer grass,
and seem to myself to need little to make me die.

Sappho

For the Courtesan Ch'ing Lin

To the tune 'The Love of the Immortals'

On your slender body
Your jade and coral girdle ornaments chime
Like those of a celestial companion
Come from the Green Jade City of Heaven.
One smile from you when we meet,
And I become speechless and forget every word.
For too long you have gathered flowers,
And leaned against the bamboos,
Your green sleeves growing cold,
In your deserted valley:
I can visualize you all alone,
A girl harboring her cryptic thoughts.

You glow like a perfumed lamp
In the gathering shadows.
We play wine games
And recite each other's poems.
Then you sing 'Remembering South of the River'
With its heart breaking verses. Then
We paint each other's beautiful eyebrows.
I want to possess you completely –
Your jade body
And your promised heart.
It is Spring.
Vast mists cover the Five Lakes.
My dear, let me buy a red painted boat
And carry you away.

Wu Tsao

translated by Kenneth Rexroth and Ling Chung

On the Road to the Sea

We passed each other, turned and stopped for half an hour, then
went our way,
I who make other women smile did not make you –
But no man can move mountains in a day.
So this hard thing is yet to do.

But first I want your life: – before I die I want to see
The world that lies behind the strangeness of your eyes,
There is nothing gay or green there for my gathering, it may be,
Yet on brown fields there lies
A haunting purple bloom: is there not something in grey skies
And in grey sea?
I want what world there is behind your eyes,
I want your life and you will not give it me.

Now, if I look, I see you walking down the years,
Young, and through August fields – a face, a thought, a
swinging dream perched on a stile –;
I would have liked (so vile we are!) to have taught you tears
But most to have made you smile.

To-day is not enough or yesterday: God sees it all –
Your length on sunny lawns, the wakeful rainy nights –; tell me –;
(how vain to ask), but it is not a question – just a call –;
Show me then, only your notched inches climbing up the garden
wall,
I like you best when you were small.

Is this a stupid thing to say
Not having spent with you one day?
No matter; I shall never touch your hair
Or hear the little tick behind your breast,
Still it is there,
And as a flying bird
Brushes the branches where it may not rest
I have brushed your hand and heard
The child in you: I like that best.

So small, so dark, so sweet; and were you also then too grave
and wise?
Always I think. Then put your far off little hand in mine; –
Oh! let it rest;
I will not stare into the early world beyond the opening eyes,
Or vex or scare what I love best.
But I want your life before mine bleeds away –
Here – not in heavenly hereafters – soon, –
I want your smile this very afternoon,
(The last of all my vices, pleasant people used to say,
I wanted and I sometimes got – the Moon!)

You know, at dusk, the last bird's cry,
And round the house the flap of the bat's low flight,
Trees that go black against the sky
And then – how soon the night!

No shadow of you on any bright road again,
And at the darkening end of this – what voice? whose kiss? As if
you'd say!
It is not I who have walked with you, it will not be I who take
away
Peace, peace, my little handful of the gleaner's grain
From your reaped fields at the shut of day.

Peace! Would you not rather die
Reeling, – with all the cannons at your ear?
So, at least, would I,
And I may not be here
To-night, to-morrow morning or next year.
Still I will let you keep your life a little while,
See dear?
I have made you smile.

Charlotte Mew

Passion

Some have won a wild delight,
By daring wilder sorrow;
Could I gain thy love to-night,
I'd hazard death to-morrow.

Could the battle-struggle earn
One kind glance from thine eye,
How this withering heart would burn,
The heady fight to try!

Welcome nights of broken sleep,
And days of carnage cold,
Could I deem that thou wouldst weep
To hear my perils told.

Tell me, if with wandering bands
I roam full far away,
Wilt thou to those distant lands
In spirit ever stray!

Wild, long, a trumpet sounds afar;
Bid me – bid me go
Where Seik and Briton meet in war,
On Indian Sutlej's flow.

Blood has dyed the Sutlej's waves
With scarlet stain, I know;
Indus' borders yawn with graves,
Yet, command me go!

Though rank and high the holocaust
Of nations steams to heaven,
Glad I'd join the death-doomed host,
Were but the mandate given.

Passion's strength should nerve my arm,
Its ardour stir my life,
Till human force to that dread charm
Should yield and sink in wild alarm,
Like trees to tempest-strife.

If, hot from war, I seek thy love,
Darest thou turn aside?
Darest thou then my fire reprove,
By scorn, and maddening pride?

No – my will shall yet control
Thy will so high and free,
And love shall tame that haughty soul –
Yes – tenderest love for me.

I'll read my triumph in thine eyes,
Behold, and prove the change;
Then leave, perchance, my noble prize,
Once more in arms to range.

I'd die when all the foam is up,
The bright wine sparkling high;
Nor wait till in the exhausted cup
Life's dull dregs only lie.

Then Love thus crowned with sweet reward,
Hope blessed with fulness large,
I'd mount the saddle, draw the sword,
And perish in the charge!

Charlotte Brontë

To the fair Clarinda, who made Love to me, imagin'd more than Woman

Fair lovely maid, or if that title be
Too weak, too feminine for nobler thee,
Permit a name that more approaches truth,
And let me call thee, lovely charming youth.
This last will justify my soft complaint,
While that may serve to lessen my constraint;
And without blushes I the youth pursue,
When so much beauteous woman is in view.
Against thy charms we struggle but in vain,
With thy deluding form thou giv'st us pain,
While the bright nymph betrays us to the swain.
In pity to our sex sure thou wert sent,
That we might love, and yet be innocent:
For sure no crime with thee we can commit;
Or if we should – thy form excuses it.
For who that gathers fairest flowers believes
A snake lies hid beneath the fragrant leaves?

Thou beauteous wonder of a different kind,
Soft Cloris with the dear Alexis join'd,
Whene'er the manly part of thee would plead,
Thou tempts us with the image of the maid,
While we the noblest passions do extend:
The love to Hermes, Aphrodite the friend.

Aphra Behn

In the conventions of pastoral poetry, young women were often termed 'nymphs', and the men, their suitors, 'swains'. Cloris is a woman's name; Alexis, the name of a youth.

Hermes was a Greek god. According to the Roman poet Ovid, his liaison with Aphrodite, the goddess of love, resulted in the birth of a son, Hermaphroditus, who was later transformed into a being who possessed the physical characteristics of both sexes – a hermaphrodite.

A Moment

The clouds had made a crimson crown
 Above the mountains high.
The stormy sun was going down
 In a stormy sky.

Why did you let your eyes so rest on me,
 And hold your breath between?
In all the ages this can never be
 As if it had not been.

Mary E. Coleridge

Sinfonia Eroica

to Sylvia

My Love, my Love, it was a day in June
A mellow, drowsy, golden afternoon;
And all the eager people thronging came
To that great hall, drawn by the magic name
Of one, a high magician, who can raise
The spirits of the past and future days,
And draw the dreams from out the secret breast,
Giving them life and shape.
I, with the rest,
Sat there athirst, atremble for the sound;
And as my aimless glances wandered round,
Far off, across the hush'd, expectant throng,
I saw your face that fac'd mine.
Clear and strong
Rush'd forth the sound, a mighty mountain stream;
Across the clust'ring heads mine eyes did seem
By subtle forces drawn, your eyes to meet.
Then you, the melody, the summer heat,
Mingled in all my blood and made it wine.
Straight I forgot the world's great woe and mine;
My spirit's murky lead grew molten fire;
Despair itself was rapture.
Ever higher,
Stronger and clearer rose the mighty strain;
Then sudden fell; then all was still again,
And I sank back, quivering as one in pain.
Brief was the pause; then, 'mid a hush profound,
Slow on the waiting air swell'd forth a sound
So wondrous sweet that each man held his breath;
A measur'd, mystic melody of death.

Then back you lean'd your head, and I could note
The upward outline of your perfect throat;
And ever, as the music smote the air,
Mine eyes from far held fast your body fair.
And in that wondrous moment seem'd to fade
My life's great woe, and grow an empty shade
Which had not been, nor was not. And I knew
Not which was sound, and which, O Love, was you.

Amy Levy

Beethoven's Third Symphony was called by the composer the 'Eroica'. The second movement is a funeral march.

'Love, you wicked dog'

Love, you wicked dog
so handsome to look at,
so awkward close up
& so unfaithful to good sense.
Whoever feeds you attention
gets you, like it or not. And
all your bad habits come with
you like a pack of fleas.
Wherever I turn for peace of mind
there is the Love dog scratching
at the door of my lonesomeness,
beating her tail against the leg
of my heart
& panting all night with red breath
in my dreams.
Love dog! Get in or out
of the house of my life, stop chewing
on my belongings, the papers &
shoes of my independence.

Judy Grahn

Song (October 1969)

I love you, Mrs Acorn. Would your husband mind
if I kissed you under the autumn sun,
if my brown-leaf guilty passion made you blind
to his manly charms and fun?

I want you, Mrs Acorn. Do you think you'll come
to see my tangled, windswept desires,
and visit me in my everchanging house of some
vision of winter's fires?

I am serious Mrs Acorn, do you hear?
Forget your family and other ties,
Come with me to where there is no fear,
where we'll find summer butterflies.

I am serious Mrs Acorn, are you deaf?

Kath Fraser

Song

Occitania, thirteenth century AD

Lady Maria, in you are excellence
and true worth, delight and true loveliness,
hospitality and intelligence.
The honours you bestow, your kindliness,
your loving looks and your playful manner,
your sweet face, your noble way of speaking,
these qualities, unmatched in any other,
make me turn to you with heart unswerving.

And so I ask you that sweet indulgence
and true love, celebration and gladness
may bring me, Lady, such beneficence
that you might grant me from your graciousness
that which has most hope and joy to offer.
For in you is all my heart's desiring,
with you I have all I know of pleasure,
and for your sake often I go sighing.

And since for worth and loveliness no other
passes you, because you are outstanding,
I ask, by this song which does you honour,
you do not love one who's undeserving.

Lovely woman, whom joy and merit favour,
and fine speech, to you my lines I'm sending,
for in you are gaiety and pleasure,
and all a woman's virtues: every good thing.

Bieiris de Romans

She describes, with emphasis on not being able to leave the final touch to painting, the portrait of a Beauty

Smooth forehead, golden hair,
eyes like sapphires, arching brows,
ivory neck and faultless nose,
ruby lips, a lustrous hue,
graceful form and body fair,
snow-white fingers in whose hold
the wand of Love we see:
this celebrates Phyllis; set in gold
a foot so small, it doesn't need
a foot.

Sor Juana Inés de la Cruz

A metrical foot is part of a line of verse.

Brown Girl

In the hot gold sunlight,
    Brown girl, brown girl,
        You smile;
    And in your great eyes,
        Very gold, very bright,
            I see little bells,
        Shaking so lazily,
            (Oh! small they are) . . . . .
            I hear the bells.

. . . .

But at fawn dusk
    Brown girl, brown girl,
        I see no smile,
        I hear no bells.
    Your great eyes
    Are quiet pools;
    They have been drinking, drinking,
        All the day,
    The hot gold of sunlight.
    Your eyes spill sunlight
        Over the dusk.
    Close your eyes,
I hear nothing but the beating of my heart.

Angelina Weld Grimké

A Girl

. . . like the reddening apple,
at the tip of the topmost twig,
which the apple-pickers missed –
or no, not missed entirely;
the one they could not reach.

Sappho

EQUILIBRIST

I'm coming toward you
always
instep on the quivering wire
leaning aside
but never looking down
eyes unsmiling
immune to sleep
or hazard

I'm coming toward you

Always your pallid image leaps
behind the bars of distance
where merge sea and sky

Not setting with the sun
nor waning with the moon
your torso centaur-like
is prancing
upon my mind's rim

Fiercely taking aim
my body is a sharpened dart
of longing
coming toward you always

May Swenson

'Nothing is sweeter than love'

'Nothing is sweeter than love'

'Nothing is sweeter than love: all other delights
come second; and even honey I spew from my mouth.'
So Nossis says. And one whom Aphrodite has not kissed
does not know – listen – what kind of flowers are her roses.

Nossis

Mouths

I think of mouths of rivers in clean countries
sliding into oceans, mixing sweet and salt.
Or mouths of caves, where dark meets greater darkness
or meets starlight.
Through the mouth of a cave
one enters, to learn secrets.
Death can wait in the mouth of a cave;
the sound of running water,
crashing waves, or silence;
bright hallucinations;
answers.

Your mouth meets mine
with secrets for the giving;
tongue meeting tongue
we taste each other's silence.
Questions. Darkness. Answers.

Jan Sellers

'I HAD BEEN HUNGRY, ALL THE YEARS'

I had been hungry, all the Years –
My Noon had Come – to dine –
I trembling drew the Table near –
And touched the Curious Wine –

'Twas this on Tables I had seen –
When turning, hungry, Home
I looked in Windows, for the Wealth
I could not hope – for Mine –

I did not know the ample Bread –
'Twas so unlike the Crumb
The Birds and I, had often shared
In Nature's – Dining Room –

The Plenty hurt me – 'twas so new –
Myself felt ill – and odd –
As Berry – of a Mountain Bush –
Transplanted – to the Road –

Nor was I hungry – so I found
That Hunger – was a way
Of Persons outside Windows –
The Entering – takes away –

Emily Dickinson

On a Night of the Full Moon

I

Out of my flesh that hungers
and my mouth that knows
comes the shape I am seeking
for reason.
The curve of your waiting body
fits my waiting hand
your breasts warm as sunlight
your lips quick as young birds
between your thighs the sweet
sharp taste of limes.

Thus I hold you
frank in my heart's eye
in my skin's knowing
as my fingers conceive your flesh
I feel your stomach
moving against me.

Before the moon wanes again
we shall come together.

II

And I would be the moon
spoken over your beckoning flesh
breaking against reservations
beaching thought
my hands at your high tide
over and under inside you
and the passing of hungers
attended, forgotten.

Darkly risen
the moon speaks
my eyes
judging your roundness
delightful.

Audre Lorde

'Come slowly – Eden!'

Come slowly – Eden!
Lips unused to Thee –
Bashful – sip thy Jessamines –
As the fainting Bee –

Reaching late his flower,
Round her chamber hums –
Counts his nectars –
Enters – and is lost in Balms.

Emily Dickinson

Summer Rain

All night our room was outer-walled with rain.
Drops fell and flattened on the tin roof,
And rang like little disks of metal.
Ping! – Ping! – and there was not a pin-point of silence between
them.
The rain rattled and clashed,
And the slats of the shutters danced and glittered.
But to me the darkness was red-gold and crocus-coloured
With your brightness,
And the words you whispered to me
Sprang up and flamed – orange torches against the rain.
Torches against the wall of cool, silver rain!

Amy Lowell

from CONTRADICTIONS: TRACKING POEMS

3

My mouth hovers across your breasts
in the short grey winter afternoon
in this bed   we are delicate
and tough   so hot with joy we amaze ourselves
tough   and delicate   we play rings
around each other   our daytime candle burns
with its peculiar light   and if the snow
begins to fall outside   filling the branches
and if the night falls   without announcement
these are the pleasures of winter
sudden, wild and delicate   your fingers
exact   my tongue exact at the same moment
stopping to laugh at a joke
my love   hot on your scent   on the cusp of winter

Adrienne Rich

Touching

The trees have been warding the sun in their boughs.
Veiled like a woman, calling to mind times past,
The twilight goes by, weeping . . . And my fingers
Follow, quivering, the outline of your thighs.

My subtle fingers loiter on the tremors
Of your flesh, under the robe soft as petals . . .
The art of touching, complex and curious, equals
The trance of perfumes, the miracle of sounds.

Slowly I follow the contour of your thighs,
Your shoulders, your neck, your unassuaged breasts.
Refined, my desire holds back from embraces;
It strokes and is ravished with innocent joys.

Renée Vivien

Riddle Game

for Mog

It is a tower on a wooded hill.
Below, a secret well seeps elixir.
Unicorns drink there.

It is the crest on a strange creature.
Watch as it rears and stiffens.
The mouth opens slowly, like a rose.

It is a dolphin in a troubled sea,
leaping and turning.
The waves are full of weed; they taste of salt.

It is the mouthpiece of a deep recorder
mellow in tone, and vibrant.
Touch the hole with your finger: hear the note vary.

It is a ridge of folded rock
over a cave with glistening walls.
There are earthquakes in that country.

Gillian Spraggs

'There comes a change in her breath'

There comes a change in her breath,
  A change that saith
She is breathing in her sleep,
Breathing, breathing and yet so low:
O life at ebb, O life at flow,
  Her life, her breath!

Michael Field
(Katharine Bradley and Edith Cooper)

'Drawing You, Heavy with Sleep . . .'

Drawing you, heavy with sleep to lie closer,
Staying your poppy head upon my shoulder,
It was as though I pulled the glide
Of a full river to my side.

Heavy with sleep and with sleep pliable
You rolled at a touch towards me. Your arm fell
Across me as a river throws
An arm of flood across meadows.

And as the careless water its mirroring sanction
Grants to him at the river's brim long stationed,
Long drowned in thought, that yet he lives
Since in that mirroring tide he moves,

Your body lying by mine to mine responded:
Your hair stirred on my mouth, my image was dandled
Deep in your sleep that flowed unstained
On from the image entertained.

Sylvia Townsend Warner

When My Love Lay Sleeping . . .

When my love lay sleeping,
it was not I,
it was the sun who splashed her
with sticky honey.
The sun
put it there. I merely watched,
patiently.
And it was the air,
mistaking her breasts
for gentle hills,
or, not mistaking at all,
but finding
a landscape so pleasing and rare,
who caressed her,
sleeping.
And it was the grass.
Its flickering tongues licked
at her feet,
crept up her thighs
and played
with her hair.
Oh it was the lascivious grass
that made my love sigh
and show herself
to me.

Suniti Namjoshi

Well!
I've always wondered
how those Nigerian sistahs
did move in those tight-ass skirts!
My skirt
flares out
from below my knee – so I could still
twis' an' shout
flash my leg through the slit
split on my left side

But y'know which part of me feels confined?
Well!
In this skirt I will not be slow-dancing
with some nice-looking sistah
we will not sit face-to-face
her knee my knee
between each other's legs
fingers tracing patterns on the inside of my thigh
making me hold my breath
and count to ten

We will not dance
legs entwined sending the pulse of the music
holding each other with legs and arms
bodies tightly together
I will not
open your legs wide wid mine
caan mek she hip-bone grine wid mine
I will not wear the bruises of such passion

I will not be lying back
vunerable in surrender in anticipation
of your mouth leaning
on me in me

Nun'na dat!
I'm bound from my wais' down
my bum and thighs held tightly together
for no woman (or man for that matter)
So how do I get my serious pleasure?
In spite of padded bra slip an' tight blouse?
will my nipples still feel
extra-sensory-perception
when they brush your full breasts?

'Nice-girls' doan sit wid d'legs open
and let the sun stream into them
warming them ouside in
doan keep d'hands pressed between their legs
hanging onto a memory –
I can still feel your tongue in me
Dancing?!
We making love
wid our close on
a sistah t'sistah art

Dorothea Smartt

A Winter's Room

The score of a song on the walls of a winter's room
dearest, the rules we broke broke open light where there was none
a fox waiting on grass, the lilacs dark and empty.
We heard the tube on tracks behind the trees
and then bells of evensong, the ropes undone, it was early
and already night had come.
            Rafted in that room . . .
if felicity was fragile as a wish, hush, a flame burnt low
with all that grey upon the land
reaching for you was to hear the light expand
till high on the frosted ceiling of the city
the birds that had not returned
were singing   your breasts lifting beneath my lips
mist torn against the blue depths of a winter
your touch erasing, warming, divining
climbing true home   as if it were a wave
as if it were the tender fall of foam   we held
and the colours ran.

A soft voice in the wind
your 'yes' that warmed the winter through.

Rhian Gallagher

Three Things

I carried two things around in my mind
Walking the woods and thinking how to say
Shiver of poplar leaves in a light wind,
Threshing of water over tumbled stones,
A brook rippling its interrupted way –
Two things that bring a tremor to the bones.

And now I carry around in my head a third.
The force of it stops me as I walk the wood,
Three things for which no one has found a word –
Wind in the poplar, tremor under the skin
Deep in the flesh, a shiver of more than blood
When lovers, water, and leaves are wholly one.

May Sarton

‘I did not live until this time’

To My Excellent Lucasia,
on our Friendship

17th July 1651

I did not live until this time
Crown'd my felicity,
When I could say without a crime,
I am not thine, but thee.

This carcass breath'd, and walk'd, and slept,
So that the world believ'd
There was a soul the motions kept;
But they were all deceiv'd.

For as a watch by art is wound
To motion, such was mine:
But never had Orinda found
A soul till she found thine;

Which now inspires, cures and supplies,
And guides my darken'd breast:
For thou art all that I can prize,
My joy, my life, my rest.

Nor bridegroom's nor crowned conqueror's mirth
To mine compar'd can be:
They have but pieces of this earth,
I've all the world in thee.

Then let our flame still light and shine,
(And no bold fear control),
As innocent as our design,
Immortal as our soul.

Katherine Philips

Lucasia was the name the poet gave to her friend Anne Owen; Orinda the name she took for herself.

PRESERVES

Only the rich ate marmalade. We had red jam
that soaked through the grey bread like blood on lint.
It might have been the war we always blamed
for everything but yet inside I knew it wasn't.

Once visiting a schoolfriend, doctor's daughter
staying the night strangely in a strange house, I looked
for it at breakfast but was only offered
honey, gilt beespit to spread on leisured toast.

This Wednesday for the first time I really made it
in your country kitchen, scalded, skinned and sliced
added white drifts of sweetness to bitter fruit
and simmered til the peel was clear as the ice

we'd played with childishly that afternoon
duck and draking the jagged panes to smithereens
on the pond's skating surface, a brittle moon
you wanted to crack. The pots gleam golden

with candied slivers aswim in a sharp sauce.
Filled with you I know I'm rich too, at last.

Maureen Duffy

MADONNA OF THE EVENING FLOWERS

All day long I have been working,
Now I am tired.
I call: 'Where are you?'
But there is only the oak-tree rustling in the wind.
The house is very quiet,
The sun shines in on your books,
On your scissors and thimble just put down,
But you are not there.
Suddenly I am lonely:
Where are you?
I go about searching.

Then I see you,
Standing under a spire of pale blue larkspur,
With a basket of roses on your arm.
You are cool, like silver,
And you smile.
I think the Canterbury bells are playing little tunes.

You tell me that the peonies need spraying,
That the columbines have overrun all bounds,
That the pyrus japonica should be cut back and rounded.
You tell me these things.
But I look at you, heart of silver,
White heart-flame of polished silver,
Burning beneath the blue steeples of the larkspur,
And I long to kneel instantly at your feet,
While all about us peal the loud, sweet *Te Deums*
of the Canterbury bells.

Amy Lowell

On Being Given Time

Sometimes it seems to be the inmost land
All children still inhabit when alone.
They play the game of morning without end,
And only lunch can bring them, startled, home
Bearing in triumph a small speckled stone.

Yet even for them, too much dispersal scatters;
What complex form the simplest game may hold!
And all we know of time that really matters
We've learned from moving clouds and waters
Where we see form and motion lightly meld.

Not the clock's tick and its relentless bind
But the long ripple that opens out beyond
The duck as he swims down the tranquil pond,
Or when a wandering, falling leaf may find
And follow the formal downpath of the wind.

It is, perhaps, our most complex creation,
A lovely skill we spend a lifetime learning,
Something between the world of pure sensation
And the world of pure thought, a new relation,
As if we held in balance the globe turning.

Even a year's not long, yet moments are.
This moment, yours and mine, and always given,
When the leaf falls, the ripple opens far,
And we go where all animals and children are,
The world is open. Love can breathe again.

May Sarton

White World

The whole white world is ours,
and the world, purple with rose-bays,
bays, bush on bush,
group, thicket, hedge and tree,
dark islands in a sea
of grey-green olive or wild white-olive,
cut with the sudden cypress shafts,
in clusters, two or three,
or with one slender, single cypress-tree.

Slid from the hill,
as crumbling snow-peaks slide,
citron on citron fill
the valley, and delight
waits till our spirits tire
of forest, grove and bush
and purple flower of the laurel-tree.

Yet not one wearies,
joined is each to each
in happiness complete
with bush and flower:
ours is the wind-breath
at the hot noon-hour,
ours is the bee's soft belly
and the blush of the rose-petal,
lifted, of the flower.

H.D.

Second Thoughts

I thought of leaving her for a day
In town, it was such iron winter
At Durdans, the garden frosty clay,
The woods as dry as any splinter,
The sky congested. I would break
From the deep, lethargic, country air
To the shining lamps, to the clash of the play,
And, to-morrow, wake
Beside her, a thousand things to say.
I planned – O more – I had almost started; –
I lifted her face in my hands to kiss, –
A face in a border of fox's fur,
For the bitter black wind had stricken her,
And she wore it – her soft hair straying out
Where it buttoned against the gray, leather snout:
In an instant we should have parted;
But at sight of the delicate world within
That fox-fur collar, from brow to chin,
At sight of those wonderful eyes from the mine,
Coal pupils, an iris of glittering spar,
And the wild, ironic, defiant shine
As of a creature behind a bar
One has captured, and, when three lives are past,
May hope to reach the heart of at last,
All that, and the love at her lips, combined
To shew me what folly it were to miss
A face with such thousand things to say,
And beside these, such thousand more to spare,
For the shining lamps, for the clash of the play –
O madness; not for a single day
Could I leave her! I stayed behind.

Michael Field
(Katharine Bradley and Edith Cooper)

Durdans was the name of the house in Reigate, Surrey, where Katharine Bradley and Edith Cooper lived between 1890 and 1899.

Regina

My Queen her sceptre did lay down,
She took from her head the golden crown
Worn by right of her royal birth.
Her purple robe she cast aside,
And the scarlet vestures of her pride,
That was the pride of the earth.
In her nakedness was she
Queen of the world, herself and me.

My Queen took up her sceptre bright,
Her crown more radiant than the light,
The rubies gleaming out of the gold.
She donned her robe of purple rare,
And did a deed that none may dare,
That makes the blood run cold.
And in her bravery is she
Queen of herself, the world and me.

Mary E. Coleridge

The Other

For you are the dervish in my valley.
Flying out your hushing skirts encompass
the windsong of wheat and barley.
Your dusty bare feet
stamp out the poppy'd ditches.
Heel toe, arms spread,
clothed in mist or sunstream,
the cadence of my days.

For you are the salmon leaper
in my headlong flood. Stretching, flashing.
The deep undershimmer of my still riverbottom.
The smooth pebble
cool in my desert mouth.

For you are the secret
caverns in my slumbrous mountain chain.
The cloud shadows,
the falcon's killing stoop along my slopes.
My creaking glaciered scour to the sea.
My clay stopped, hoarded fountaining.

For you are the flame
on my hour candle.
My rhythms, circadian, lunar,
all resolve in your counterbeat.
The green unfolding,
the flamboyant flowering,
in my seasons' turning.
The reaper at my pained harvest,
the sower at my rebirth.

Barbara Burford

A Love Song

Like a wave that roams the sea,
So lonely and so free,
Like a cloud that haunts the sky,
So distant and so high,
Like the fragrant summer wind,
So gentle and so kind,
Like a lily by the wall,
So golden and so tall,
Gay as any flower that blows,
Splendid as a sun-lit rose,
Bright and bravely blossoming,
Is my Lady of the Spring.
Fair of face, and clear of sight,
Living always in the light,
Valorous and free and strong
As the wind's courageous song,
All of magic sunshine made,
Secret as a forest glade,
Silver-lit beneath dark trees
By pale-starred anemones,
Fair as that white dawn that gleams
Through the ivory gate of dreams,
Glorious to gaze upon,
With strange lights of summers gone,
Silver of bright daisies stored,
Smallest change in summer's hoard,
Gold of vanished daffodils,
Is my Lady of the Hills.

The grace of all things gay,
The joy of a swallow's flight,
The light of a summer's day,
The peace of a moon-lit night,
All the strength, and the hope, and the gladness of living are hers,
And her voice is the voice of the wind in a forest of firs.

Eva Gore-Booth

To the Well-Beloved

You are my palace, my evening and my autumn,
And my sail of silk and my garden of lilies,
My censer of gold and my white column,
My parkland, and my pool, with its reeds and its iris.

You are my perfumes of amber and honey, my palm,
My leafy boughs, the cicadas' song on the breeze,
My snow that murders itself in hauteur and calm,
And my sea-wrack and my vistas of the seas.

And you are my bell that sobs with unvarying tone,
My airy island and my saving oasis . . .
You are my palace, my evening and my autumn,
And my sail of silk and my garden of lilies.

Renée Vivien

THE LADY AND THE UNICORN

The Cluny Tapestries

I am the unicorn and bow my head
You are the lady woven into history
And here forever we are bound in mystery
Our wine, Imagination, and our bread,
And I the unicorn who bows his head.

You are all interwoven in my history
And you and I have been most strangely wed
I am the unicorn and bow my head
And lay my wildness down upon your knee
You are the lady woven into history.

And here forever we are sweetly wed
With flowers and rabbits in the tapestry
You are the lady woven into history
Imagination is our bridal bed:
We lie ghostly upon it, no word said.

Among the flowers of the tapestry
I am the unicorn and by your bed
Come gently, gently to bow down my head,
Lay at your side this love, this mystery,
And call you lady of my tapestry.

I am the unicorn and bow my head
To one so sweetly lost, so strangely wed:

You sit forever under a small formal tree
Where I forever search your eyes to be

Rewarded with this shining tragedy
And know your beauty was not cast for me,

Know we are woven all in mystery,
The wound imagined where no one has bled,

My wild love chastened to this history
Where I before your eyes, bow down my head.

May Sarton

'I LOVE YOU WITH MY LIFE – 'TIS SO I LOVE YOU'

I love you with my life – 'tis so I love you;
    I give you as a ring
The cycle of my days till death:
    I worship with the breath
That keeps me in the world with you and spring:
And God may dwell behind, but not above you.

Mine, in the dark, before the world's beginning:
    The claim of every sense,
    Secret and source of every need;
    The goal to which I speed,
And at my heart a vigour more immense
Than will itself to urge me to its winning.

Michael Field
(Katharine Bradley and Edith Cooper)

Affection

The earth that made the rose,
She also is thy mother, and not I.
The flame wherewith thy maiden spirit glows
Was lighted at no hearth that I sit by.
I am as far below as heaven above thee.
Were I thine angel, more I could not love thee.

Bid me defend thee!
Thy danger over-human strength shall lend me,
A hand of iron and a heart of steel,
To strike, to wound, to slay, and not to feel.
But if you chide me,
I am a weak, defenceless child beside thee.

Mary E. Coleridge

‘A CREATURE BITTER-SWEET, BAFFLING’

'Once more Love stirs me up'

Once more Love stirs me up, the limb-loosener,
a creature bitter-sweet, baffling.

Sappho

Region of No Birds

Where the earth groans with earthquake
I know you,
Where the waters boil black
And the dragons are
You are immersed in me.
Beyond pleasure, where terror is kissed
And the small I's die.

In that region of no birds
One does not speak prettily of love.

Elsa Gidlow

Close

Lock the door. In the dark journey of our night,
two childhoods stand in the corner of the bedroom
watching the way we take each other to bits
to stare at our heart. I hear a story
told in sleep in a lost accent. You know the words.

Undress. A suitcase crammed with secrets
bursts in the wardrobe at the foot of the bed.
Dress again. Undress. You have me like a drawing,
erased, coloured in, untitled, signed by your tongue.
The name of a country written in red on my palm,

unreadable. I tell myself where I live now,
but you move in close till I shake, homeless,
further than that. A coin falls from the bedside table,
spinning its heads and tails. How the hell
can I win. How can I lose. Tell me again.

Love won't give in. It makes a hired room tremble
with the pity of bells, a cigarette smoke itself
next to a full glass of wine, time ache
into space, space, wants no more talk. Now
it has me where I want me, now you, you do.

Put out the light. Years stand outside on the street
looking up to an open window, black as our mouth
which utters its tuneless song. The ghosts of ourselves,
behind and before us, throng in a mirror, blind,
laughing and weeping. They know who we are.

Carol Ann Duffy

Four Beginnings/for Kyra

1. You raise
   your face from mine, parting
   my breath like water, hair falling
   away in its own wind, and your eyes –
   green in the light like honey – surfacing
   on my body, awed
   with desire, speechless, this common dream.

2. You bore your marriage like a misconceived
   animal, and have the scars, the pale
   ridged tissue round front and back
   for proof. For proof. Tonight

   we cross into each other's language. I take your hand
   hesitant still with regret
   into that milky landscape, where braille
   is a tongue for lovers, where tongue,
   fingers, lips
   share a lidless eye.

3. I was surprised myself – the image of the lithe
   hermaphroditic lover a staple of
   every fantasy, bought, borrowed, or mine. We never did
   mention the word, unqualified: I love:
   your hair, I love: your feet, toes, tender nibbles, I love:

   I love. You are the memory
   of each desire that ran, dead-end, into a mind
   programmed to misconstrue it. A mind inventing
   neurosis, anxiety, phobia, a mind expertly camouflaged
   from the thought of love
   for a woman, its native
   love.

4. I in my narrow body, spellbound
   against your flesh.

Olga Broumas

from A PURE LOVE, ONE WHICH IS FROM A DISTANCE AND DOES NOT LUST AFTER INDECENCIES, IS ABLE TO FEEL WHATEVER THE MOST PROFANE LOVE FEELS

. . . I, my beloved Phyllis,
who worship you as a goddess,
who venerate your rigour,
and idolize your disdain:
I am like the foolish lover
who, seeking to touch the brightness,
turning blindly in circles,
becomes a prey to the flame;
just like the innocent child
who rashly applies his fingers
to the edge of the knife, misled
by the brightness of the steel,
and his tender hand is cut;
yet, failing to grasp his error,
sharper than the pain of the wound
he feels the confiscation;
like the sunflower, sick with love,
who, following her lover,
the red-gold father of lights,
wishes to teach him to glow;
as air to a vacant space,
as fire to what it consumes,
as rocks that fall to the ground,
as intentions seeking their goal;
just like all things in nature,
who wish to preserve their existence,
and so they unite in loving,
and link in intimate bonds . . .

But why exhaust the theme?
For yourself, Phyllis, I love you;
this is just amplification
of what your merits deserve.
Being a woman, and remote,
is not an impediment;
for souls, as you are aware,
do not know distance nor sex.

(ll.77–112)

Sor Juana Inés de la Cruz

Body Language

The thing that makes me crazy is
how much I wanted her –
the simple act of longing
year after year, till finally
she took my hand and held it
pressed to her small right breast.
That kind of longing
turns your whole torso into a cavern
where despair echoes wall to wall
and hope leaps like a foetus.
My complicity confuses the issue.
How to say the word: *abuse*
when my body tells another story –
not a tale of clenched self-protection
but an epic, my young arm
reaching out for her breast,
my back spreading wide to her touch?

The thing I go back to is
the rain on the window –
water washing all over the pane
as hand moves to breast
and someone seduces someone else.
My complicity clouds the definitions
like that misted window,
one side of its thin old glass
steaming with the heat of breath and skin
while the other
leans into the storm, weeping.

Judith Barrington

A Modern Naiad

The swirls of the sea used to gleam in your dress.
Your body was like the treacherous tide that slips away.
You would draw me towards you as a chasm draws water;
Your flexible hands had the lure of the net,
And your wandering hair would float on your breast
Tenuous and fluid as ocean weed.

That deceptive allure which adorns danger
Gave yet more sweetness to your fickle smile;
Your forehead brought to mind the tranquil deeps,
And the song of the sirens sang to me from your eyes.

Renée Vivien

A Mona Lisa

I

I should like to creep
Through the long brown grasses
That are your lashes;
I should like to poise
On the very brink
Of the leaf-brown pools
That are your shadowed eyes;
I should like to cleave
Without sound,
Their glimmering waters,
Their unrippled waters,
I should like to sink down
And down
And down . . . . .
And deeply drown.

II

Would I be more than a bubble breaking?
Or an ever-widening circle
Ceasing at the marge?
Would my white bones
Be the only white bones
Wavering back and forth, back and forth
In their depths?

Angelina Weld Grimké

White Wolf

I found your short white hairs
in my bed and laid them side by side.

Four bright hairs on one black sheet
I wanted a fifth for a cross stroke.

I wanted the blood from between your legs
to make communion. I fished it out, dragged

stripes down your flanks to make a rite
to keep you coming back to my bed.

But when you came you were loose and howling,
you cried all night and called me names.

In your sharp brown teeth was a year's debris
so close, you said, bone close.

The next time you came they found us out
and your armpits like swallows couldn't comfort me,

not your smile like a snake's, the slope of your eyes,
your long mouth gone cold to the tongue.

A tree grew up through the floor of my room
and we hung upside down from its branches.

And the next time you came you didn't come at all,
you gave yourself back to the bridebox

your aromatic fur turned nylon, you
crawled back in with a twig in your teeth

lay still, and flapped your lids shut.

Christina Dunhill

Words Without Echo

Come then
forget that you saw it
forget that I said it,
forget the cold truths
that have come between us like glass.

Forgive the body
that has such different things to say
and only one way to say them.
Forget the old luxuries:
words without echo
eyes with no reflection.

Come then
– many flowers blossom on one stem
kiss me,
and I will not ask
why you close your eyes.

Mary Dorcey

ANNA/MARGARET

You are the answer to all my riddles,
the master-key to my cipher.
Each rhyme is in relation to your name,
sometimes the sequence of consonants,
sometimes the tune of vowels. The breaks
between stanzas are shaped by your absence.
Each image connects with the next because
you are between them. My found poems
are constructed from your old letters,
your shopping lists, your memoranda.

If I laid out a garden it would include a maze;
in the centre a space only you could fill.
My stage sets would demand you make an entrance.
My songs would be set for your voice.
In my tapestry your initials form the border
entwined with daisies and peacocks.

My pictures would be painted with your colours –
blues, greens, the sheen of feathers.
My abstracts based on the geometry of your body,
parabola of breast, angle of hip, strong
upthrust of hair. The way I apply pigment
corresponds to your gestures, incisive,
erratic, impulsive. The relationship between forms
traces what was once between us.

Your name patterns my landscape, spelled out
in white stones you can only see from the air
or once a year, for a few minutes, at dawn,
at the time of the solstice. In a dry year
the foundations of our lives together
show up in pale markings.

But I read your books as they are published,
haunt your garden, attend your exhibition,
watch your performance, echo your song,
unpick the strands of your embroidery,
fly over your bleak country
and I can find no sign of how it was.

Or how it was we became strangers.

Dorothy Nimmo

Margaret/Anna

When she left there were traces of her
in the upstairs drawers. Hairpins. Pencil stubs.

I made sure I cleaned them away.
The sight of them made me oddly nervous.

I felt she had taken possession and indeed
there was a time when I felt possessed.

There has to be some give and take
between friends. I gave her what I had available:

coffee, banana bread. She refused both;
it was something else she wanted

and that I sometimes fear she took.
Because when she left there were things missing.

I've removed all evidence of our relationship,
whatever it may have been, from my records.

I don't read what she writes for fear I might
understand it. I don't open her letters.

I don't remember her. And I would tell her so
but I have lost her address.

Dorothy Nimmo

Armida's Garden

I have been there before thee, O my love!
   Each winding way I know and all the flowers,
The shadowy cypress trees, the twilight grove,
   Where rest, in fragrant sleep, the enchanted hours.

I have been there before thee. At the end
   There stands a gate through which thou too must pass.
When thou shalt reach it, God in mercy send
   Thou say no bitterer word, love, than 'Alas!'

Mary E. Coleridge

Armida was a beautiful sorceress in the Italian epic poem *Gerusalemme liberata* by Torquato Tasso (1575). She charmed the knight Rinaldo into falling in love with her.

When the Lights Go Up

You promise a beginning, like the smooth
opening of the long, dark drapes
in the cinema, which whisper
'I will take all your pain away'.

When I hear your red Rover
change into third at the bottom of our hill
it seems to growl like the MGM lion,
'I will make you insatiable'.

You laugh when I haven't been funny,
your laugh, smoky as Talisker,
and feed me salted popcorn
glazed with butter and gunpowder.
Your eyes burn and flicker,
'I will show you a good time'.

You bathe me in rosemary,
wrap me in a thick blanket of new skin
and call softly from a black and white film
'You are the most beautiful thing
I have ever seen'.

I could almost feel the ground slip
your palm settle on my brow,
taste your melted chocolate
almost eat your baked vanilla buns
believe you when you say
'Believe me'.
But when the phone rings after midnight
I let it ring.

Cherry Smyth

'I lie alone'

'The Moon has sunk'

The Moon has sunk
and the Pleiades;
midnight is here,
the hour goes by,
I lie alone.

attributed to Sappho

'Bitter rain in my courtyard'

To the tune 'The Joy of Peace and Brightness'

Bitter rain in my courtyard
In the decline of Autumn,
I only have vague poetic feelings
That I cannot bring together.
They diffuse into the dark clouds
And the red leaves.
After the yellow sunset
The cold moon rises
Out of the gloomy mist.
I will not let down the blinds
Of spotted bamboo from their silver hook.
Tonight my dreams will follow the wind,
Suffering the cold,
To the jasper tower of your beautiful flesh.

Wu Tsao

translated by Kenneth Rexroth and Ling Chung

Sonnet XXXIII

June 1780

Last night her form the hours of slumber bless'd
Whose eyes illumin'd all my youthful years. –
Spirit of dreams, at thy command appears
Each airy shape, that visiting our rest,
Dismays, perplexes or delights the breast.
My pensive heart this kind indulgence cheers;
Bliss, in no waking moment now possess'd,
Bliss, ask'd of thee with memory's thrilling tears.
Nightly I cry, – how oft, alas! in vain, –
Give, by thy powers, that airy shapes control,
Honora to my visions! – ah! ordain
Her beauteous lip may wear the smile that stole,
In years long fled, the sting from every pain!
Show her sweet face, ah, show it to my soul!

Anna Seward

On the Threshold

O God, my dream! I dreamed that you were dead;
Your mother hung above the couch and wept
Whereon you lay all white, and garlanded
With blooms of waxen whiteness. I had crept
Up to your chamber-door, which stood ajar,
And in the doorway watched you from afar,
Nor dared advance to kiss your lips and brow.
I had no part nor lot in you, as now;
Death had not broken between us the old bar;
Nor torn from out my heart the old, cold sense
Of your misprision and my impotence.

Amy Levy

Parting with Lucasia

13th January 1658
A song

Well! we will do that rigid thing
Which makes spectators think we part;
Though absence hath for none a sting
But those who keep each other's heart.

And when our sense is dispossess'd,
Our labouring souls will heave and pant,
And gasp for one another's breast,
Since their conveyances they want.

Nay, we have felt the tedious smart
Of absent friendship, and do know
That when we die we can but part;
And who knows what we shall do now?

Yet since I must go, we'll submit,
And so our own disposers be;
For while we nobly suffer it,
We triumph o'er necessity.

By this we shall be truly great,
If, having other things o'ercome,
To make our victory complete
We can be conquerors at home!

Nay then to meet we may conclude,
And all obstructions overthrow;
Since we our passions have subdued,
Which is the strongest thing I know.

Katherine Philips

The Taxi

When I go away from you
The world beats dead
Like a slackened drum.
I call out for you against the jutted stars
And shout into the ridges of the wind.
Streets coming fast,
One after the other,
Wedge you away from me,
And the lamps of the city prick my eyes
So that I can no longer see your face.
Why should I leave you,
To wound myself upon the sharp edges of the night?

Amy Lowell

Away from You

This isn't a memory. It is something I am doing.
Something I always do when I am not with you.
I repeat everything; and it happens to me again.
You pull down the zip of my jacket. Kiss me.
Especially, in this place, in this weather.
The rain shining the big slabs of stone
outside the old mill house. The trapped hill
opposite moves like a large animal in heat.
I walk across its back; while you get into a red car
in a foreign town. It is probably raining there.
Splashing you, as the door opens for you.
I lose you in the traffic. I panic.
Your car crashes. I am at your funeral.
There's the long low wail of the organ.
I see my own death happen before my eyes.
I am in this other place, waiting. This is longing.
Going on. Your voice lodged inside my head.

No. You are in the house in the foreign town.
Looking out of the window. I have seen that look
on your face. You have that look on your face.
Now. I climb the stairs slowly to the bed,
the first bed, and you, waking, take me.
Outside the rain runs across the animal's aching back.
Later, in your time, the rain leaves the dusty town.

Jackie Kay

A Love-Letter

Bavaria, twelfth century AD, original in Latin

To G –, her only rose,
From A –, a bond of precious love, sent to the one she chose.
Where shall I find the courage to go on,
the patience to endure it, now that you are gone?
Have I the endurance of a stony block,
to wait till you come back?
Day and night I grieve without an end,
like one who lacks foot and hand.
All that should bring me joy and delight,
without you, feels like mud, fit to be trodden underfoot.
In place of happiness the tears come,
my spirit seems to feel a perpetual gloom.
When I recall the kisses you impressed
upon my mouth, and how with words of joy you stroked my little breasts,
I want to die,
because I am not allowed to see you.
What shall I do, I that am sadder than any?
Where shall I turn, I that am poorer than any?
O that my body had been trusted to the keeping of the ground
until that longed-for time when you are homeward bound,
or that, like the prophet Habakkuk, it were granted to me once
to travel to that place in a trance,
so that I might look upon the face of my lover,
and then I should not care if I died that same hour!
For in all the world there is no woman born
who is so lovable, with so much charm,
nor one who, without deception,
loves me with such adoration.

And so my endless lamentations will not cease
until I gain the sight of your face.
Truly, to quote from a certain sage, it is for anyone a great misery
not to be with that without which he cannot be.
For so long as the world shall endure,
you shall never be erased from my heart's core.
But why do I patter on?
Sweet love, return!
Do not delay your journey any longer,
Keep in mind that I cannot bear your absence any further.
Goodbye,
remember me.

A –

'She thought you were like a goddess revealed in splendour'

[She thought] you were like a goddess revealed in splendour,
and found in your singing her deepest delight,

but now she is conspicuous among the Lydian women
as, when the sun sets, the rose-fingered Moon

subdues all the stars. She throws her light
alike across the salty sea and over flowering fields.

A beautiful dew is poured down, and the roses flourish,
the delicate chervil and the flowering clover.

And often, as she wanders, remembering gentle Atthis,
desire gnaws in her slender breast and pain eats out her heart.

Sappho

Orinda to Lucasia

Observe the weary birds ere night be done,
How they would fain call up the tardy sun,
With feathers hung with dew,
And trembling voices too,
They court their glorious planet to appear,
That they may find recruits of spirits there.
The drooping flowers hang their heads,
And languish down into their beds;
While brooks more bold and fierce than they,
Wanting those beams from whence
All things drink influence,
Openly murmur, and demand the day.

Thou, my Lucasia, art far more to me
Than he to all the underworld can be;
From thee I've heat and light,
Thy absence makes my night.
But ah! my friend, it now grows very long,
The sadness weighty, and the darkness strong:
My tears (its dew) dwell on my cheeks,
And still my heart thy dawning seeks,
And to thee mournfully it cries,
That if too long I wait,
Ev'n thou may'st come too late,
And not restore my life, but close my eyes.

Katherine Philips

The Spindle: Lament for Baucis

GIRLS: Torty-tortoise, what are you doing in the middle of the ring?
TORTOISE: (*scuttling from side to side*) I am weaving wool and Milesian weft.
GIRLS: And what was your son doing when he was lost?
TORTOISE: From the white horses into the sea he SPRANG!

On the last word the Tortoise jumps up to chase the other girls; the first one to be caught becomes the new Tortoise.

Girls' game recorded by Julius Pollux of Naucratis,
second century AD

This poem has survived in only a very fragmentary state. Ellipses indicate a missing word or series of words, while the words in square brackets are doubtful or conjectural.

. . . into the wave
[you sprang] from the white horses with crazy bounds.
"Aiai!" I screamed. [Then it was my turn to be] tortoise,
and leaping up, [I raced] through the pen in the great courtyard.
Unlucky Baucis! this is why . . . I mourn for you,
and in my heart . . . these traces still lie warm.
Now, they are only embers, those things [we used to share]:

of dolls . . . in our chambers . . . brides . . . towards dawn
[my/your] mother . . . woolworkers . . . about the cloth shot with purple

Ah! [in those days] the bogey-woman [so] frightened [us two] little ones:
. . . on her head she had [huge] ears,
and she roamed around on four feet;
she would change her appearance [from one thing to another].

But when the time came that [you went to your marriage] bed,
you forgot all the things which while you were still a child
. . . you had heard from your mother, dear Baucis:
. . . Aphrodite [put] forgetfulness [in your heart].
So, crying out for you . . . the rest I set aside.
For my feet [are] not [so] profane [as to leave] the house,
nor [is it fit that I should] set eyes on your [corpse],
nor lament with my flowing hair uncovered . . .
the regard I feel for you crimsons my [cheeks] and tears them.

. . . always in the past . . . nineteen . . . Erinna . . . dear [girls] . . .
looking at a spindle . . . know that to you . . . spinning round . . .
for this reason my regard . . . unmarried girls . . . perceiving . . .
and flowing hair . . .

Gray-headed women, gentle in speech, who are the flower of old
age among mortals

. . . you dear . . . O Baucis! . . . weeping . . . a flame . . . hearing
howling . . . O Hymen! . . . O Hymen! . . . Aiai! unlucky Baucis! . . .

From here to Hades an echo swims vainly across;
silence among the dead; the darkness flows over my eyes.

Erinna

Hymen was a god who was invoked at weddings.

‘Faithful and sweet was our love, Biote’

Gravestone, late fifth century BC, Athens

Faithful and sweet was our love, Biote,
and so your lover, Euthylla, set this stone upon your grave.
In the prime of your life, you wasted away.
Her tears fall endlessly, and she cries aloud,
holding your memory always in her mind.

Euthylla (?)

On the death of that most excellent lady, the Marquise de Mancera

May they die with you, Laura, since you have died,
these impotent desires that long for you,
these eyes, deprived of what they yearn to see,
a lovely light that once on them you shed.
May it die, my luckless lyre, that cries in pain
where once it echoed your inspiring voice,
and may the ill-formed scrawlings of my verse
be like black tears that fall from my sad pen.
May Death herself be moved to pity you,
since, bound by rule, she could not spare your life,
and Love against his bitter fortune cry
that though before this time he longed to have
eyes, so your lovely form he might enjoy,
now they shall serve him only to weep his grief.

Sor Juana Inés de la Cruz

Cupid, the god of love, was sometimes depicted as blind.

IN APRIL

I am come to the threshold of a spring
Where there will be nothing
To stand between me and the smite
Of the martin's scooping flight,
Between me and the halloo
Of the first cuckoo.
'As you hear the first cuckoo,
So you will be all summer through.'
This year I shall hear it naked and alone;
And lengthening days and strengthening sun will show
Me my solitary shadow,
My cypressed shadow – but no,
My Love, I was not alone; in my mind I was talking with you
When I heard the first cuckoo,
And gentle as thistledown his call was blown.

Sylvia Townsend Warner

A Miracle

How gladly I would give
My life to her who would not choose to live
If I should die!
Death, when thou passest by,
Take us together, so I sigh,
Praying and sighing through the London streets
While my heart beats
To do some miracle, when suddenly
At curve of Regent Circus I espy,
Set 'mid a jeweller's trays of spangle-glitter,
A tiny metal insect-pin, a fly.
This utter trifle for my love I buy,
And, thinking of it on her breast,
My heart hath rest.

Michael Field
(Katharine Bradley and Edith Cooper)

'Love, love, the dogs are after me'

The Hare

Love, love, the dogs are after me,
I am transmuted to a white hare.
You sit in the lighted house and cannot see,
I know that you are there.
See where I pass, a shadow on the grass,
Come swiftly
Lift me to your care.

Anna Wickham

Saturday Market

Bury your heart in some deep green hollow
        Or hide it up in a kind old tree
Better still, give it the swallow
        When she goes over the sea.

In Saturday Market there's eggs a 'plenty
        And dead-alive ducks with their legs tied down,
Grey old gaffers and boys of twenty –
        Girls and the women of the town –
Pitchers and sugar-sticks, ribbons and laces,
        Posies and whips and dicky-birds' seed,
Silver pieces and smiling faces,
        In Saturday Market they've all they need.

What were you showing in Saturday Market
        That set it grinning from end to end
Girls and gaffers and boys of twenty –?
        Cover it close with your shawl, my friend –
Hasten you home with the laugh behind you,
        Over the down –, out of sight,
Fasten your door, though no one will find you
        No one will look on a Market night.

See, you, the shawl is wet, take out from under
        The red dead thing –. In the white of the moon
On the flags does it stir again? Well, and no wonder!
        Best make an end of it; bury it soon.
If there is blood on the hearth who'll know it?
        Or blood on the stairs,
When a murder is over and done why show it?
        In Saturday Market nobody cares.

Then lie you straight on your bed for a short, short weeping
    And still, for a long, long rest,
There's never a one in the town so sure of sleeping
    As you, in the house on the down with a hole in your breast.

Think no more of the swallow,
    Forget, you, the sea,
Never again remember the deep green hollow
    Or the top of the kind old tree!

Charlotte Mew

WORDS TO MY LOVE

You understand me: I am a middling creature,
Not good, nor very bad, peaceable, a bit sly.
I hate heavy perfumes, or a sudden outcry,
And grey I prize dearer than scarlet or ochre.

I love the fading day, which bit by bit dies down,
A fire, the closed-in intimacy of a chamber
Where the lamps, dimming their panes of yellow amber,
Redden the old bronze and tinge with blue the freestone.

My eyes on the carpet, which is smoother than sand,
Idly I evoke the shores of golden peas,
Where the brightness of lovely times long past still drifts . . .
And yet, in spite of this, I bear the sinner's brand.

See: I am at the age when the virgin yields her hand
To the man her weakness makes her seek out and dread,
And I have not chosen a comrade for the road,
Because you appeared at a place where the path turned.

On the hills the hyacinth was bleeding crimson,
You were in a dream, and Eros walked beside you . . .
I am a woman, I have no right to beauty.
They have condemned me to the ugliness of men.

I had the unforgivable impudence to ask
For the love of sisters, which is delicate and pure,
The stealthy footstep that leaves the ferns without scar,
And the gentle voice that comes to blend with the dusk.

They have forbidden me your hair, your eyes,
Because your hair is long and scented with odours,
And because your eyes have in their depths strange ardours,
And are turbulent like the uncontrollable seas.

They have wagged their fingers in an offended way,
Because my gaze was seeking out your tender gaze . . .
No one has wished to understand, watching us pass,
That I have, in all simplicity, chosen you.

Contemplate the disgraceful law that I transgress
And judge my love, which is ignorant of evil,
As guileless, necessary and inevitable
As the desire that joins the lover and the mistress.

They did not read the brightness in my eyes at all,
As I walked the path my destiny led me on,
And they said to each other, 'Who is that doomed woman
Who is secretly devoured by the flames of Hell?'

Let us leave them to take care of their tainted morals,
And let us dream that the dawn is honey-flaxen,
That the day without bitterness, the night without spleen
Are coming, just like friends whose kindliness consoles . . .

We shall go to see the starlight on the heights together . . .
What does it matter to us – to us – the judgement of men?
And what is there for us to fear, since we remain
Pure in the eyes of life, and we love each other? . . .

Renée Vivien

Lines 10 and 17 contain allusions to Sappho, Fragments 143 and l05c.
Eros is the Greek god of love.

The Transgress

That summer midnight under her aurora
northern and still we passed the barrier.

Two make a curse, one giving, one accepting.
It takes two to break a curse

transformed at last in each other's eyes.

I sat on the naked bed of space,
all things becoming other than what they seem

in the night-waking, in the revelation
thundering on tabu after the broken

imperative, while the grotesque ancestors fade
with you breathing beside me through our dream:

bed of forbidden things finally known –
art from the symbol struck, living and made.

Branch lifted green from the dead shock of stone.

Muriel Rukeyser

Private Love

Becoming a lesbian gave me a voice
And took away my tongue.

I am a professional lady –
Acceptable;
I am a predatory pervert –
Shocking;
Efficient, disruptive, reliable, abnormal –
I introduce clients,
I seduce women.

By day I wear a dress
Coolly answer telephones.
I sleep rough at night
Hot in another's bed.

My lover knows hard wisdom
Learnt from silences in public,
Where unsettled voices
Piss abuse –
'What d'ya call that, mate?
Is it a girl, or a geezer?'

'At times like this,' she says,
'I wish I had a submachine gun.'

I watch my quiet and beautiful terrorist
Despised, pick herself up
Become a woman again.

Our private love trembles to be enough
Where no rituals reward our desire;
Shy and weary we battle
For how we are
And map out shorter, safer routes
Through forbidden territories
Which grow large,
More dangerous.

Yet before us pass proud lovers
Who will still come,
Will grace our sheets
Move wet for our touch.
Their renascent hopes
Crowd our rooms –
They strengthen me.

For now we hold fast and fierce to love
Beyond the cry of early passion,
It hurts to catch the heart
On sharp, unfinished compromise.

Cherry Smyth

We Can Compose Ourselves

We can compose an ocean if we like;
deck it about with sand dunes, a
mountain or two, some trees.
Or we can compose ourselves.
But a politics? To invent, just we two,
a view? How to think? What to do?
And a country?
                                        In yours, though the
climate is warm, the buildings fabulous,
though even the rocks have names,
we wither, having no word.
                                                            And in mine,
the word is so raw it bleeds; and from
fury of pain, it attacks; and would
maim us daily. We can compose ourselves;
but it's our bodies, not our passports,
fit so uncommonly well.

Suniti Namjoshi and Gillian Hanscombe

'It was deep April, and the morn'

It was deep April, and the morn
        Shakspere was born;
The world was on us, pressing sore;
My Love and I took hands and swore
    Against the world, to be
Poets and lovers evermore,
To laugh and dream on Lethe's shore,
To sing to Charon in his boat,
Heartening the timid souls afloat;
Of judgment never to take heed,
But to those fast-locked souls to speed,
Who never from Apollo fled,
Who spent no hour among the dead;
        Continually
        With them to dwell,
Indifferent to heaven and hell.

Michael Field
(Katharine Bradley and Edith Cooper)

Lethe is one of the rivers of the underworld in Greek mythology and Charon the ferryman who carries the souls of the dead in his boat.
Apollo is the god of poetry and music.

We Press Buttons

Yesterday on the beach
in an erogenous zone
we had a 90s experience
in black and white

Swam naked in
the champagne froth of the sea
and fell back onto
black crushed velvet sand
like the night that came upon us
like drunkenness

The moon
lit up the contours of the night
pulled back the tide
too hot for covers
we rolled on this relentless bed until
we slept like starfish
in perfect shadow

Today technicolour dawn
breaks the champagne bottle
leaving no romantic message

Thick frothy scum
throws up
bright supermarket packaging
multi-coloured used condoms
strange sea creatures

Someone on the promenade stares at
our black and white held hands and
in daylight colour becomes an issue

God in his designer
blue and white polka dot tie
admires the upward curves on
the company profit chart
lights a thick yellow cigar and
sinks deep into a plump office chair
pleased with his creation

The almost red desert sand
is consumed with tents and tanks
on all channels

We press buttons
hoping to escape
in black and white adverts

Patience Agbabi

Going Under

I turn over pages, you say,
Louder than any woman in Europe.

But reading's my specific for keeping
Reality at bay; my lullaby.

You slip into sleep as fast
And neat as a dipper.
You lie there breathing, breathing.

My language is turn over
Over and over again. I am a fish
Netted on a giveaway mattress,
Urgent to be out of the air.

Reading would help; or pills.
But light would wake you from your resolute
Progress through night.

The dreams waiting for me twitter and bleat.
All the things I ever did wrong
Queue by the bed in order of precedence,
Worst last.

Exhausted by guilt, I nuzzle
Your shoulder. Out lobs
A casual, heavy arm. You anchor me
In your own easy sound.

U. A. Fanthorpe

'You sleep now, my self in your arms'

You sleep now, my self in your arms,
My weight lies smooth, heavy
Between your breasts and thighs.
Homeless my thoughts wander the city,
Walk the waters of Thames,
Light as others' dreams.

Feel that quick touch?
That was my mouth on yours.

Ghost, unfleshed since you hold my substance
I am all air and fire;
All water too, liquefy in tears
Like classic heroes who wept unashamed
At love or fate.

'Why out so late?' They stop me
In the street, shine torches in my eyes.
Revenant, unhoused I stammer blind.
'No fixed abode?' Their notebooks poise.
Tell them I have a lodging close at hand;
Surety, bond; that doors stand wide for me
And, with daylight, you will take me in.

Maureen Duffy

The Road to Kerity

Do you remember the two old people we passed on the road to
Kerity,
Resting their sack on the stones, by the drenched wayside,
Looking at us with their lightless eyes through the driving rain,
and then out again
To the rocks, and the long white line of the tide:
Frozen ghosts that were children once, husband and wife, father
and mother,
Looking at us with those frozen eyes; have you ever seen anything
quite so chilled or so old?
But we – with our arms about each other,
We did not feel the cold!

Charlotte Mew

Song

Your spirit is my treasury,
My storehouse and my armoury.
There rich, bright stuffs are found
And rare sweet foods abound
With curious knives designed to slay
Those prowlers of the night and day
Who ate my noon and took my sleep,
And held me captive in my keep.
Now in your being I can move,
My air, my path, my light, my love!

Anna Wickham

Deserted House

Knowing the house deserted, amid the darkness of trees
That seemed to my memories
Flat as vernal scenery upon a stage,
Greatly daring I came to the house again;
Came straight, for I knew its intimacies;
Broke through bracken and wood to the tower with the weather
vane;
Came to visit the place
I thought not to visit again.

And knowing the secret ways between tree and tree,
I came through undergrowth
To the falling folly once more,
Where we played together, my brother and I, and he
Who died by his own hand, another brother to me.
But the folly had gone; and down I kneeled on the floor
That remained, a great slab of stone, the tombstone of three.

And the ghosts rose up: children who trotted beside
Me, a child again. But alone I had not died.

And that day I feared the deserted house, and the brake,
The trees and the glades of the wood,
I feared the forsaken garden,
For none of the living were there, and another ghost,
He who gave me life (and his spirit I feared the most),
Walked, silent, for ever alone alongside the lake,
Whom no living woman had understood.

I came yet a second time to that house and garden,
With the one whom I love, saying: 'Come, let us enter the house,
That I feared so before to do.'

And we climbed by a window and stood
On the old blank landing I knew,
Where, a child, on the stairway to bed,
In a corner I huddled alone to look at the stars,
Where first the awe and fear of infinity took me.
We went up the hollow stairs and after us followed the dead.
In the empty nursery I cried: 'There, there was the bed,
Where she beat me and shook me,
When I cried with terror at night.'

Then the one whom I love
Held me long on that spot, held me deep,
Murmuring: 'Here is the healing,
Here is the answer, the pardon.'
Since when I play with ghosts in the house and the garden,
In dreams,
When asleep.

* * *

But my love took another love
New Year when the snow was deep.

So I came a third time,
Like a leveret over the snow,
To stand at the roots of the nursery lime,
Where the squares of the windows were leaden,
Not golden as long ago.
And I knew that the children played
With drum and painted toys,
Whilst our favourite, the suicide, walked the landing;
Now the ghosts were I and the boys –

The boys that cook brown trout with me
On the fire in the folly, in dreams,
So the tramp says: 'The hares
Have been here again, it seems.'

Dorothy Wellesley

Restless Dialogue

What do you see, honey,
Tell me what you see.
I see this passion dwindled to a pinpoint,
Pinpoint, swordpoint, a knife for stabbing.

What do you hear, honey,
Tell me what you hear.
I hear a crowd mobbing a delicate secret,
The race-law shouted and the lynch-cross hammered.

But I am here, honey,
Feel me, I am here.
Yes, you are here, with your volcano tenderness,
Running tongue of lava to enfold but not harm me.

Close as can be, honey,
Our bodies are close.
But also are drumskins stretched many miles around us,
Heels beat upon us a tattoo of anger.

They cannot find us, honey,
Not if we are quiet.
Maybe not find us, maybe be quiet,
Maybe be strangled in straitjacket quiet.

What do you want, honey,
Tell me what you want.
Anything but lie here, anything but listen.
Swordpoint, knife-edge, at last turn outward.

Naomi Replansky

from Twenty-One Love Poems

XIII

The rules break like a thermometer,
quicksilver spills across the charted systems,
we're out in a country that has no language
no laws, we're chasing the raven and the wren
through gorges unexplored since dawn
whatever we do together is pure invention
the maps they gave us were out of date
by years . . . we're driving through the desert
wondering if the water will hold out
the hallucinations turn to simple villages
the music on the radio comes clear –
neither *Rosenkavalier* nor *Götterdämmerung*
but a woman's voice singing old songs
with new words, with a quiet bass, a flute
plucked and fingered by women outside the law.

Adrienne Rich

'THE BEAUTY AND LIGHT OF THE SUN'

‘But I love the richness of things’

But I love the richness of things . . . and to me
Love has apportioned a share in the beauty and light of the sun.

Sappho

Women at the Lakeside

The light! The light on this water
Has not been seen by
men;
This is women's light.
From their sister element it reflects
eyes
Blue, green or grey, algae-brown;
The lake's single eye
one with them.

It takes their floating hair,
Playing, as with its own water plants,
Strands brown, black, gold
Undulate with the lily pads.

As they float, fluid, given
To their liquid past
The immersed bodies shimmer,
Ripple with their laughter,
and
Small fishes nibble, curious
tentative,
Testing nipples pink or brown;
(Fish? Fly? Bug? Bud of flower?)
From fingers moving as fins
The minnows dart, –
Splinters of watery light.

At the moist lake marge
Sun warmed, wave lipped,
The women touch, merge
limbs with limbs
Flowing together
In love cool as
kiss of wavelet.

Knowing themselves of earth,
Air, fire, thought-in-formed,
This day they resolve
All to water, to memory
Of light on water,
The human burden
                                                  sinking
as a stone.

The light! Oh, the light on this water
Will not be seen by men.

Elsa Gidlow

'SOME SAY IT'S A FORCE OF CAVALRY'

Some say it's a force of cavalry, others of foot,
others of ships, but I say that the most beautiful thing
upon the black earth is whatever it is you desire.

It's easy enough to make this plain to all:
for she who was far more beautiful than any woman of mortal
race,
Helen, abandoned her husband – the best of men –

and went sailing off to Troy; she remembered neither her child
nor her much-loved parents, but [Aphrodite]
led her astray . . .

[This] has made me think of Anactoria, who isn't here.

Her step, which stirs desire, and the bright sparkle of her face,
are dearer sights to me than the chariots of Lydia,
and armed men fighting on foot.

Sappho

16

It's like breathing this love: it comes
so easy to me. It breaks into smiles
laughter at shared childish jokes
or sight of you coming downstairs
or last always through the barrier
afraid I won't be there
a childhood fear I inherit
from that portmanteau you bring with you
and open for me to show the dress
puffsleeved with a cherry on the pocket
you were bought postwar holidaying
on roller skates through another country
a Victorian child strayed
into movieland where the rules were drawn back.
I try to pull them aside now
to show our sea prospect but my need
makes me clumsy. I want you
rollercoastering hand in mine
down this freeway where we only have to
catch our breath to kiss and never stumble.

Maureen Duffy

7301

Learning to read you, twenty years ago,
Over the pub lunch cheese-and-onion rolls.

Learning you eat raw onions; learning your taste
For obscurity, how you encode teachers and classrooms

As *the hands, the shop-floor*; learning to hide
The sudden shining naked looks of love. And thinking

The rest of our lives, the rest of our lives
Doing perfectly ordinary things together – riding

In buses, walking in Sainsbury's, sitting
In pubs eating cheese-and-onion rolls,

All those tomorrows. Now twenty years after,
We've had seventy-three hundred of them, and

(If your arithmetic's right, and our luck) we may
Fairly reckon on seventy-three hundred more.

I hold them crammed in my arms, colossal crops
Of shining tomorrows that may never happen,

But may they! Still learning to read you,
To hear what it is you're saying, to master the code.

U. A. Fanthorpe

In the Seventh Year

for Louise

Our sea is still mysterious as morning mist
its flapping arms stretched out for dry sand
its running heels sliding over pebbles
when the sun dives in at night

We are turquoise and clear some days
still as breeze; others stormy like stones
you are in deep stroking my bones
my love an ache, the early light

spreading the water
seven years seven years I repeat
over and over
clasping this timeless, this changing thing.

Jackie Kay

Idyll

Your voice and your footsteps fall soft as dew on my working day.
Where I sit there is spring in the air around me from your living warmth.
You flower in my thought, you flower in my blood, and I wonder only
that my happy hands do not blossom into heavy roses.

Now the space of the everyday closes around us two, like a soft, gentle mist.
Are you afraid of becoming a prisoner, are you afraid of drowning in the greyness?
Do not be afraid: in the everyday's innermost depth,
in the heart of all life,
there burns with quietly humming flames a deep, secret festival.

Karin Boye

translated by David McDuff

from Sybil: The Glide of Her Tongue
The Prophetical Songs

2

She whom I honour, honoured me. Therefore I
speak. Disregard all rumours you may have heard.
I never speak in riddles: that's simply what men
hear.

(Oh, she is agile, strong-handed, supple and
insistent. She is handsome. She shines in the dark.
My breasts fall by themselves into her hands.)

Love

is a discipline, she told me; and must be learned.

3

In the guise of Artemis, hunter, you can ride me all
the way to the sun; and be ridden back again. Your
bow-arm is stronger than an olive-stump, though
your hands are as smooth as plums. When you pour
libations, my ears sting with the brim and swish of
your words. I adore the bowstring pulled taut; the
symptoms of desire.

8

By rule of thumb I come gracefully, bearing gifts.
There is thrift in the teasing, prudence in pleasing,
restraint in remembrance of passion.

I glance and

glitter; I laugh the laugh of cut glass.

As I leave the bed

I remark how you see me lose glamour, gain gravity.

11

After we'd decided, we made promises. And after that, we kept them. And after that came the failures. Then we got down to it: mapped each other's flaws, and confessed to chivalry. And then, because of all that, we made love with our bare hands. Outside, the pigeons pecking at the moss on the roof, were also contented.

Gillian Hanscombe

Enclosures

Better than anything, I like
your ordinary occupations
to be different from mine.

At night, on either side
of this scrubbed table, set
with food I've cooked,

on plates you've washed,
you do your crossword,
I'll read my book: both

rinsed in the same clean
river of music. Daily
we pile our separate stones

on drystone walls enclosing
private places. You hedge
my bets. I mend your fences;

but going down to the bone,
love is finger printed with distance;
your grain's your own.

Kate Foley

The Heron

The heron watched the water; I watched you,
poised like the heron on the mooring wall.
You watched the heron watch the river flow.
We waited, silently. And that was all
till the great bird leaned out, in the mauve-grey light,
shifted its feet, stretched shadowed wings, took flight.
Wings creaked over us, steadied, gliding high,
skimmed clear of trees. A landscape tilting by.

I have watched you do the same, on a mountainside;
bend to the fell's own rhythm, with a stride
long-legged and lean, that eases miles away
not for the destination, but the path, the way
itself, ambiguous then clear
and you the walker, and belonging there
till the April evening settles, dark and chill
calling you down at last from the silent fell.

Jan Sellers

A Decade

When you came, you were like red wine and honey,
And the taste of you burnt my mouth with its sweetness.
Now you are like morning bread,
Smooth and pleasant.
I hardly taste you at all for I know your savour,
But I am completely nourished.

Amy Lowell

from LETTERS FROM MAINE

7

Who has spoken of the unicorn in old age?
She who was hunted for her strangeness,
Androgynous, fleeing her pursuers, hopeful
When she was young that she could bow her horn
Before the perfect innocence and purity
Of a virgin being. Who has wondered
Whether she did find shelter at last?
Or does she wander still, searching human faces
For the one who might speak of her
In her own language, look into her eyes
And gentle the wildness once and for all?
It may be that through that fervent pursuit
The unicorn has come to look for wisdom
And experience rather than innocence,
That she looks for a woman who has suffered
And become like gold, the dross beaten out,
As round and whole as a wedding ring,
A woman who has laughed and wept her way
Through the dark wood and across the lake,
Who has borne children, and who is now
Marvelously open, transparent, and unafraid.
Who has imagined the unicorn grown old?

May Sarton

In That Particular Temple

In that particular temple
a god slept
and a goddess danced,
and in another
a goddess slept and a god
danced.
Do I dare say it? Perhaps –
it is possible –
that it's all the same?
That rapt
and dispassionate stare,
the flaring curve
of the gorgeous hip
and the round
and unashamed breasts,
I have worshipped
before. When we make love
you and I
are both sacred and secular.
The goddess's limbs
begin to move.
Balanced underfoot
the world spins.

Suniti Namjoshi and Gillian Hanscombe

'There are never enough love poems'

There are never enough love poems
for you whose lips swell and darken
to burgundy   black grapes   garnets
your scent   the smell of the sea

the rhythm of your heartbeat
the tidal surge of waves
all one in this white room above the beach

sunlight on crumpled pillows
warming skin as silk
as granite polished by Atlantic storms

beyond the open windows
the curve of downlands   misted   wet with rain

Jan Sellers

BIOGRAPHICAL NOTES

A – is all the identification we have for an unknown woman, probably a nun, who wrote a love-letter to another woman, probably also a nun, in irregular Latin rhyming verse. This love-letter is the second of two very similar compositions preserved in the same manuscript. The manuscript was compiled between about 1160 and 1186; it comes from the monastery of Tegernsee in Bavaria and is now in Munich.

Patience Agbabi is a London-based internationally renowned performance poet. She is published in several anthologies, including *The Virago Book of Wicked Verse* (1992). Her first collection, *R.A.W.*, was published by Gecko Press in 1995. Since then she has collaborated with Adeola Agbebiyi and **Dorothea Smartt** to create *FO(U)R WOMEN*, a polyvocal performance piece which was premièred at the ICA in May 1996. She is also a member of Britain's first poetry pop group, Atomic Lip. She is currently working on a second book, a collection of erotic poetry.

Judith Barrington is a poet and memoir writer. She is the author of two volumes of poetry: *Trying to be an Honest Woman* (1985) and *History and Geography* (1989). Her most recent book is *Writing the Memoir: From Truth to Art* (The Eighth Mountain Press, 1997). She directs the Flight of the Mind Writing Workshops for Women and is president of Soapstone: A Writing Retreat for Women. She teaches at writing workshops all over the USA and has provided the librettos for two full-length musical works. In 1997 she and her partner of nineteen years, Ruth Gundle, received the Stuart H. Holbook Award from Literary Arts Inc. for outstanding contributions to Oregon literary life.

Aphra Behn (*c.* 1640–89) was a prolific dramatist, poet and novelist, and has been described as the first English woman to take up writing as a profession. She was married briefly to a merchant of Dutch or German extraction and had several lovers. She lived for a while in the Dutch West Indies, and also in Holland, where she acted as a spy for the government of Charles II. Several of her poems hint at a sexual interest in women; 'To the fair Clarinda' is the most explicit of these, and the wittiest.

Bieiris de Romans is a shadowy figure who probably lived in the first half of the thirteenth century. 'Bieiris' is a form of the name Beatrice. The town of Romans is in southern France, in the département of Drôme. Nothing else is known about her, except that her sole surviving poem, a love-song written to another woman, the equally shadowy Lady Maria, is unique in the traditions of the troubadour lyric. The original text of her poem, in Provençal, may be found in Meg Bogin's book *The Woman Troubadours* (Paddington Press, 1976), which also contains the best introduction to the woman troubadours and their society.

Karin Boye (1900–1941) was born in Göteborg, Sweden, and studied at Uppsala and Stockholm universities. She was interested in psychoanalysis and spent several months in Berlin in 1932, undergoing analysis. She worked as a journalist and from 1936 as a teacher. Although she was briefly married, in her late twenties, most of her important relationships were with women. Her novel *Crisis* (1933) deals with her adolescent discovery of her bisexuality. Several other novels were published as well as five books of poetry, one posthumously. She committed suicide in 1941.

Charlotte Brontë (1816–55) is best known for her novels, but her earliest work to appear in print was in the collection of poems that was published by her and her sisters Anne and Emily in 1846. The poem included in this anthology, 'Passion', appeared in that collection. Charlotte's lifelong passionate friendship with Ellen

Nussey is documented by Elaine Miller in *Not a Passing Phase: Reclaiming Lesbians in History 1840–1985* (The Women's Press, 1989, reprinted and updated 1993).

Olga Broumas (b. 1949) is Greek by birth, but in *c.* 1968 migrated to the USA where she studied architecture at the universities of Pennsylvania and Oregon. Her second book of poems, *Beginning with O* (1977), was chosen for the Yale Younger Poets Award. She has published several later volumes, some of them collaborative, and translated the poems of the modern Greek poet Odysseus Elytis. Founder of Freehand Inc., a community of women artists, she has taught English, Women's Studies and Creative Writing, and has worked as a massage therapist and a musician. Recently she has been poet-in-residence at Brandeis University.

Barbara Burford (b. 1945) is a poet, dramatist and short-story writer. A selection of her poems appeared in *A Dangerous Knowing: Four Black Women Poets* (Sheba, 1985), alongside work by **Jackie Kay**, and she has co-edited a collection of poetry for The Women's Press, *Dancing the Tightrope: New Love Poems by Women* (1987). Her play, *Patterns*, was performed in 1984 at The Drill Hall, and at the Oval Theatre. *The Threshing Floor* (Sheba, 1986) contains short stories and a novella.

Mary E. Coleridge (1861–1907) was the daughter of a comfortable middle-class home. Remaining unmarried, she lived with her parents all her life. Her emotional and intellectual life centred on a group of close women friends, and some of her poetry is strongly homoerotic in feeling. She published relatively few poems during her life, and those under the pen-name 'Anodos', since she was sensitive about seeming to challenge comparison with Samuel Taylor Coleridge, who was her great-great-uncle. She also wrote several novels, which were published under her own name.

Emily Dickinson (1830–86) was born, educated and lived her life in Amherst, Massachusetts, the daughter of a US congressman. In the course of a life of growing seclusion, she wrote a huge number of poems. Very few of these were published during her lifetime, and those few were edited by others to conform with standard notions of punctuation and metre. She addressed herself passionately in poems and letters to two of her women friends, Sue Gilbert, who became her sister-in-law, and Kate Scott Anthon, to whom she had a brief but very intense attachment.

Mary Dorcey (b. 1950) is a short-story writer, novelist and poet. Born in County Dublin, Ireland, she has been active in the Women's Movement since 1972 and was a founder member of Irish Women United and the Irish Gay Rights Movement. She has published two collections of poetry; her work has been frequently anthologized, and performed on stage, radio and television. She has led creative writing workshops in Ireland and England since 1982.

Carol Ann Duffy (b. 1955) comes originally from Glasgow. She has published four collections of poetry and has had plays produced on stage and radio. Her many awards include first prize in the 1983 National Poetry Competition, a Somerset Maugham Award in 1988, the 1989 Dylan Thomas Award and a Cholmondeley Award in 1992. The publication of *Mean Time* in 1993 won her the Forward and Whitbread poetry prizes. She lives in Manchester with her daughter.

Maureen Duffy (b. 1933) was born in Worthing, Sussex and educated at King's College, London. A novelist, playwright, poet and biographer, her numerous publications include several collections of poetry, and her *Collected Poems 1949–1984* was published in 1985. She has written a biography of **Aphra Behn** and introductions to several volumes of Behn's work. Lesbian identity is a key theme of her novel *The Microcosm* (1966). She is a past president of the Writers' Guild of Great Britain.

Christina Dunhill teaches creative writing at the City Literary Institute, London, and in private workshops. She has edited an anthology of women's poetry, *As Girls Could Boast* (Oscars Press, 1994). Her poems have appeared in the *Observer*, *Verse*, *The North*, *The Rialto*, *Poetry London Newsletter* and in several anthologies, including *Jugular Defences*, an AIDS anthology (Oscars Press, 1994). She was a finalist for the Arvon Prize in 1993 and is working on a first collection.

Erinna probably lived at the end of the fourth century BC on the Greek island of Telos. Her major work, *The Spindle*, is a lament for her childhood friend and lover, Baucis, who died very suddenly, immediately after her marriage. Erinna is said to have written it as an unmarried girl of nineteen years, and to have composed it while working at her spindle and loom. The original poem consisted of 300 hexameter lines, but only fragments have survived.

Euthylla lived in Athens at the end of the fifth century BC. Her gravestone for Biote (the 'o' is short, the 'e' long) was found in the burial ground which was in the part of the city called the Kerameikos, to the north-west of the Acropolis. The inscription was published by Werner Peek in *Griechische Vers-Inschriften I: Grab-Epigramme* (Akademie-Verlag, 1955), no. 1415.

U. A. Fanthorpe (b. 1929) was born in Kent and educated at St Anne's College, Oxford. She taught for sixteen years at Cheltenham Ladies' College, before becoming 'a middle-aged drop-out' in order to write. She is now a full-time writer. In 1994 she became the first woman poet to be nominated for the post of Oxford Professor of Poetry. She has published six collections of poems; her latest, *Safe as Houses*, appeared in 1995.

Michael Field was the pen-name used by Katharine Bradley (1846–1914) and Edith Cooper (1862–1913). Bradley, who was educated at Newnham College, Cambridge, was Cooper's aunt and helped to bring her up. They collaborated on twenty-seven poetic tragedies and a number of volumes of poetry, choosing a male pseudonym to gain wider acceptance for their work. They were lovers (they saw their relationship as a superior form of marriage), and their work includes a number of love poems addressed to each other. They lived together throughout their lives, and died within a few months of each other, of cancer. Two of the poems in this anthology, 'Second Thoughts' and 'A Miracle', were published posthumously in 1923.

Kate Foley (b. 1938) was brought up in North West London where she went to a convent grammar school. She has been a nurse and a midwife, and before retiring was head of a national laboratory for conservation and archaeometry. Her first collection, *Soft Engineering*, was published by Onlywomen Press in 1994. Her work has appeared in many magazines and anthologies and she hopes to bring out another collection shortly.

Kath Fraser was unable to settle on a single version of her life and accepted her lover's offer to write one. 'Kath is fifty now, and not the same person at all, in many ways, as the one who wrote "Song (October 1969)". Then, she was a new lesbian, intense and unsure of herself, prone to having strange parties and writing poetry to drinking cronies. Now, she's growing into the real power of just simply being herself. She meditates, makes sculptures, does t'ai chi, practises as a psychologist, enjoys long walks in the local countryside, and conversation with her eccentric lover. A well-rounded life! She even writes poetry, occasionally.'

Rhian Gallagher was born in New Zealand and has lived in London for the past ten years. She currently works as a press officer for a fine arts publisher. Her poetry has been published in literary magazines in the UK and New Zealand, including *Stand*, *The Rialto*, *Poetry New Zealand* and *Poetry London Newsletter*.

Elsa Gidlow (1898–1986) was born in Hull, but emigrated to Quebec with her family when she was six. In 1921 she moved to New York City and in 1923 published *On a Grey Thread*, the first openly lesbian volume of poetry to be published in North America. In the mid-1920s she moved to San Francisco and for the rest of her life she made her home in the California Bay area. She published several further volumes of poems, while earning her living as a freelance journalist. Her autobiography, *Elsa: I Come with My Songs* (Booklegger Press, 1986), is a remarkable document of lesbian life in the decades before the Women's Movement.

Eva Gore-Booth (1870–1926) was born in Ireland to an Anglo-Irish landowning family. In 1896 she met Esther Roper, a feminist activist, and the two soon became, in Roper's words, 'friends and companions for life'. By 1897 Eva Gore-Booth had settled in Manchester, where she dedicated herself to work for women. She was active in the trade union movement, as well as the women's suffrage movement. During the First World War, she worked for the Women's Peace Crusade, and from 1916 for the cause of Irish independence. She published several volumes of poetry and several verse plays, some of which were acted. Much of her poetry is mystical, some of it drawing on Irish heroic legend. 'A Love Poem' is a very early poem. Two lines which are noticeably inferior to the rest have been removed in this reprint. These are lines seven and eight in the original: 'Like a castle in the air, / So joyous and so fair'.

Judy Grahn (b. 1940) is an American poet and fiction writer, born in Chicago and brought up in New Mexico. At the age of twenty-one she was expelled from the US air force for being a lesbian. Her early poems were collected in *The Work of a Common Woman*, with an introduction by **Adrienne Rich** (St Martin's Press, 1978). Since then she has published two poetry sequences based on the tarot suits, *The Queen of Wands* (1982) and *The Queen of Swords* (1987). She has also published short stories, a fantastic novel and works of speculative cultural history. Her book *Another Mother Tongue: Gay Words, Gay Worlds* (Beacon Press, 1984) contains much autobiographical material.

Angelina Weld Grimké (1880–1958) was born in Boston, Massachusetts. Her father, a lawyer, was the son of a black slave; her mother, who was white, left home when Angelina was a baby. A leading figure in the Harlem Renaissance of the 1920s, she wrote poems, plays and short stories, but seems to have stopped writing after her father died in 1930. As early as fourteen, she was writing love-letters to women and her lesbian desires are expressed in a number of her poems, but to please her father she resolved to deny herself the fulfilment of them. A selection from her work, including a number of her poems, was edited by Carolivia Herron in 1991, but many poems remain in manuscript.

H.D. was the pen-name of Hilda Doolittle (1886–1961). American by birth, educated at Bryn Mawr, she married an Englishman, Richard Aldington, in 1913. Her first collection of poems, *Sea Garden*, was published in 1916. At this time she was associated with Ezra Pound's Imagist movement, which also attracted **Amy Lowell**. By the end of the war her marriage had collapsed. In 1919 she gave birth to a daughter, Perdita, and began her lifelong relationship with the novelist Bryher (Winnifred Ellerman). 'White World' was published in her second collection, *Hymen* (1921), which was dedicated to Bryher and Perdita. A prolific writer, drawn to experiment, her work includes – in addition to poetry – novels, short stories, essays and autobiography; some of her published work appeared posthumously.

Gillian Hanscombe (b. 1945) comes from Melbourne, Australia, but has lived in England since 1969. She has a son, and together with Jackie Forster has written a book, *Rocking the Cradle*, on lesbian mothers. Her other books include a feminist satire, *Figments of a Murder* (1995), which is part crime novel, part political inquiry, and two sequences of prose poems, *Sybil: The Glide of Her Tongue* (1992) and *The Interloper* (1996). *Flesh and Paper* (1986), written with **Suniti Namjoshi**, is a sequence of poems that forms a dialogue between two lesbian lovers. The authors live together in Devon, where Gillian Hanscombe is director of the Centre for Women's Studies, University of Exeter. Her book *Writing for Their Lives: The Modernist Women 1910–1940* (1987), co-authored with Virginia L. Smyers, includes chapters on **H.D.** and **Amy Lowell**.

Sor Juana Inés de la Cruz (1648–1695) was born in Mexico, the illegitimate daughter of a Spanish landowner. In 1664 she became lady-in-waiting to the wife of the Viceroy, the Marquise de Mancera, whom she addresses as 'Laura' in her poems. In 1669 she became a nun. In 1680, the arrival of a new viceregal couple brought a second aristocratic patroness, the Marquise de la Laguna, whom she addresses in her poems as 'Phyllis' and 'Lysis'. The eroticism of these poems is unmistakable; its context is debated. She also wrote love poems to men. But she eventually fell foul of the Church authorities and was made to abandon her secular studies and writings. She died soon after, in an epidemic.

Jackie Kay (b. 1961) was born in Edinburgh and brought up in Glasgow. A selection of her poems appeared in *A Dangerous Knowing: Four Black Women Poets* (Sheba, 1985), alongside work by **Barbara Burford**. Her first solo collection, *The Adoption Papers* (Bloodaxe, 1991), explored her experience as a black child adopted by white parents. It received a Scottish Arts Council Book Award, a Saltire First Book of the Year Award and a Forward Prize in 1992. Her second collection, *Other Lovers*, appeared in 1993. She has also published *Two's Company* (Blackie, 1992), an award-winning collection of poems for children, and has written widely for stage and television. She lives in London.

Amy Levy (1861–89) was born in Clapham. She was the first Jewish student to study at Newnham College, Cambridge. An active feminist and radical, she was concerned about the position of women in the Anglo-Jewish community, and about the position of Jewish people in Europe. During her short lifetime she published two collections of poetry and three novels. Several of her poems are markedly homoerotic in their themes. She died by her own hand, shortly after correcting the proofs of her third, posthumously published, volume of poems.

Audre Lorde (1934–92) was born in New York to parents from Grenada. Poet and essayist, she left a fictionalised account of her early life in *Zami: A New Spelling of My Name* (1982) and an account of the beginning of her struggle with the cancer that eventually killed her in *The Cancer Journals* (1980). Her essay 'Uses of the Erotic: The Erotic as Power' (1978) proclaims the value of the erotic in women's lives as a source of political and creative power. Her many collections of poetry include *The Black Unicorn* (1978), *Chosen Poems: Old and New* (1982) and *Our Dead Behind Us* (1986). She won many awards and fellowships, and worked as a librarian and as a university English teacher.

Amy Lowell (1874–1925) was born into a wealthy New England family. She began writing poetry in 1902; her first book of poems, *A Dome of Many-Coloured Glass*, appeared in 1912. A key moment in her poetic career came in 1913, when she became aware of Ezra Pound's Imagist movement. On visits to England in 1913 and 1914 she met Pound and other Imagists, including **H.D.** In 1914 she began her lifelong relationship with the actress Ada Russell, for whom she wrote 'Madonna of the Evening Flowers' and others of her love poems. An immensely prolific poet, she produced numerous collections, including two that were published posthumously.

Charlotte Mew (1869–1928) was born in London, where she lived throughout her life. She published stories and poems in *The Yellow Book*, but broke her connection at the time of Oscar Wilde's arrest, in 1895. In 1913 she met and fell in love with the novelist May Sinclair, who was horrified by her declaration and made her the subject of cruel gossip. Her first collection of poems, *The Farmer's Bride* (1916), was published by the Poetry Bookshop. Her second, *The Rambling Sailor*, appeared the year after her death by suicide.

Suniti Namjoshi (b. 1941) was born in Bombay. From 1972 to 1987 she taught English Literature at the University of Toronto. Since 1987 she has lived in Devon with **Gillian Hanscombe**. She had published four collections of poems before, in 1981, publishing *Feminist Fables*, a collection of reworked and original fables, myths and fairy stories. Myth and fable have continued to be important in her work. *Flesh and Paper* (1986), written with Gillian Hanscombe, is a sequence of poems that forms a dialogue between two lesbian lovers. Her most recent book is *Building Babel* (Spinifex, 1996), a novel which has its own Internet site, the Babel Building Site, to which readers are invited to make contributions.

Dorothy Nimmo (b. 1932) was educated in York and Cambridge. She spent the 1950s acting in London, the 1960s having four children in Geneva and the 1970s bringing them up near Peterborough. In 1980 she was divorced and started to write. In 1989 she ran away to a Quaker Centre for Study and Contemplation in Pennsylvania and then became warden of the Friends' Meeting House in Gloucester. Now warden of the Friends' Meeting House in Settle, North Yorkshire, she has published four books of poetry. Her fifth collection, *The Children's Games*, was published by Smith/Doorstop Books in 1998. She received a Cholmondeley Award for poetry in 1996.

Nossis flourished *c.* 300 BC. An aristocrat by birth, she lived in the Dorian Greek colony of Locri, on the southern tip of Italy. Love was the dominant theme of her work and the epigram translated in this anthology was probably written as the introduction to a collection of her poems. Only twelve short poems survive and none of the others is about love. In one of them, she associates herself with the tradition of Sappho and it is very likely that her lost love poems were addressed to women.

Katherine Philips (1632–64) was born in London, the daughter of a wealthy merchant. Her family, and the husband she married in 1648, were Parliamentarians. She herself was a staunch Royalist. She took the name Orinda among her friends and most of her poems were written under this name. Many of them were poems of passionate friendship to female friends. One of the chief of these was Anne Owen, whom she addresses in her poems as Lucasia. Her poems circulated in manuscript during her lifetime; an unauthorized edition appeared at the end of her life and an authorized edition was published in 1667. She died of smallpox.

Naomi Replansky (b. 1918) was born in New York, where she still lives. She graduated in geography from the University of California, Los Angeles, in 1956. She has worked as a lathe operator, computer programmer and teacher. *Ring Song* (1952), her first collection of poems, was nominated for the National Book Award. Her most recent collection, *The Dangerous World: New and Selected Poems, 1934–1994* was published in 1994. Her poems have been published widely in journals and anthologies, and she has also published translations from German and Yiddish literature.

Adrienne Rich (b. 1929) was born in Baltimore. Since the selection of her first volume by W. H. Auden for the Yale Series of Younger Poets in 1951, her work has continually broken new ground, moving from closed forms to a feminist poetics and a radical urban imagination and politics. Her books of poetry include *Collected Early Poems 1950–1970*, *The Dream of a Common Language: Poems 1974–1977*, *Your Native Land, Your Life*, *Time's Power*, *An Atlas of the Difficult World* and *Dark Fields of the Republic*. Prose works include *Of Woman Born: Motherhood As Experience and Institution*, *On Lies, Secrets and Silence*, *Blood, Bread and Poetry* and *What is Found There: Notebooks on Poetry and Politics*. Her work has received many awards, including the Ruth Lilly Prize, the Los Angeles Times Book Award, the Lambda Literary Award, the Poets' Prize, the Lenore Marshall/Nation Award, a MacArthur Fellowship and the Dorothea Tanning Prize.

Muriel Rukeyser (1913–80) was born in New York and educated at Vassar and Columbia University. *Theory of Flight*, the first of her nineteen volumes of poetry, won a Yale Younger Poets Award in 1935. She was also a distinguished biographer and translator. A lifelong political activist, who travelled to Spain during the Civil War and later was gaoled for campaigning against the war in Vietnam, her commitment to peace and social justice is reflected throughout her work. Bisexual, she was married, briefly, in 1945, and later raised a son as a single parent. 'The Transgress' is taken from *The Speed of Darkness* (1968), the collection in which she first began to approach the theme of lesbian experience.

Sappho lived on the Greek island of Lesbos in the late seventh and early sixth centuries BC. Much of her work is lost and most of what remains is fragmentary. An aristocrat by birth, she wrote a number of poems intended for performance at weddings, as well as lyrics of an apparently personal nature, dealing with erotic friendships between women. It is clear from her surviving work that she had a personal devotion to the goddess Aphrodite, as well as to the Muses, the goddesses of poetry and music.

May Sarton (1912–95) was born in Belgium to an English mother and an American father, who took refuge in Cambridge, Massachusetts, on the outbreak of the First World War. For most of her life she lived in America. Her early career was in the theatre and she subsequently held a series of teaching jobs. Her first collection of poems was published in 1937; she continued to write and publish poetry into her eighties. Her novel *Mrs Stevens Hears the Mermaids Singing* (1974) explores the life history and reflections of a bisexual (predominantly lesbian) poet. She published numerous other novels, many of which remain in print, as well as diaries and autobiographies.

Jan Sellers works part-time at the University of Kent teaching study techniques. Among the journals in which her poems have appeared are *Critical Quarterly*, *The Rialto* and *Common Lives/Lesbian Lives* (USA). She has also published poems in a number of collections, including *What Lesbian Do in Books* (The Women's Press, 1991), *The Virago Book of Wicked Verse* (Virago, 1992), *Language of Water, Language of Fire* (Oscars Press, 1992), *Virago New Poets* (Virago, 1993) and *As Girls Could Boast* (Oscars Press, 1994).

Anna Seward (1742–1809) was the daughter of a canon of Lichfield Cathedral. She never married, but kept house for her father, a widower. It is clear that this suited her preference. She was emotionally attached to a number of women friends, but the passion that inspired many of her poems was for Honora Sneyd, nine years her junior, who was brought up virtually as her adopted sister. Honora's marriage, in 1773, distressed and angered Anna; her death, of consumption, in 1780, caused her intense grief. In 1795 she began a friendship with the Ladies of Llangollen, Lady Eleanor Butler and Sarah Ponsonby, aristocratic women famous for eloping together and for their lifelong romantic partnership. She celebrated their relationship in some of her poems.

Dorothea Smartt, daughter of Barbajan parents, is a poet and live artist. She was a 1995–6 Attached Live Artist at the Institute of Contemporary Arts, London, and has been widely commissioned.

She reads and performs at a variety of venues in Britain and abroad, including the Centre for Contemporary Art (Glasgow), the Green Room (Manchester), Audre Lorde Women's Poetry Center (New York) and Apples & Snakes poetry events. Her latest publishing credits include *Mythic Women Real Women* (Faber, 1998) and *The Fire People* (Payback Press, 1998), and she is co-editor of *Words from the Women's Café* (Centerprise, 1993). She lectures part-time with London's Birkbeck College and Leeds University. Currently she is developing new performance work and working towards her long-awaited poetry collection.

Cherry Smyth performs her work in a range of venues from cafés to cinemas and works as a journalist and film programmer. She is Irish, trying to resist assimilation living in London. Her poetry is published in *Of Eros and of Dust* (Oscars Press, 1992), *Frankenstein's Daughter* (Stride Publications, 1993) and *Virago New Poets* (Virago Press, 1993). Of her non-fiction, *Queer Notions* (Scarlet Press) was published in 1992 and *Damn Fine Art by New Lesbian Artists* (Cassell) in 1996. She is currently working on a novel and a collection of short stories, though poetry remains her first love.

May Swenson (1913–89) was born into a Mormon family in Utah but spent most of her working life in New York. She published eleven volumes of poetry, including some for children, and received many fellowships and grants. She was a chancellor of the American Academy of Poets. Lesbian themes are important in her work, but are handled circumspectly. She lived for many years with the novelist Rozanne R. Knudsen, for whom she wrote a number of poems.

Renée Vivien was the adopted name of Pauline Tarn (1877–1909), who was born in London, the granddaughter of a shopping magnate. Much of her early life was spent in France and she came to dislike England. She began to write poetry in French while she was in her teens; her first book of poems was published in 1901. Between then and her early death she produced a substantial body of poetry, including two volumes of prose poems. Her novel *Une*

Femme m'apparut (1905) is founded on her stormy affair with Natalie Barney, the expatriate American heiress and writer.

Sylvia Townsend Warner (1893–1978) was born in Harrow-on-the-Hill, where her father was a master at the public school. Her first book, *The Espalier* (1925) was a collection of poems; it was followed a year later by a novel, *Lolly Willowes*, which won her an immediate reputation. She went on to publish six more novels, ten volumes of short stories, a biography (of the novelist T. H. White) and several further collections of poetry. A lifelong partnership with the poet Valentine Ackland (1906–68) began in 1930; the two published a joint collection, *Whether a Dove or Seagull*, in 1933. Sylvia Townsend Warner's *Collected Poems* appeared in 1982, edited by Claire Harman.

Dorothy Wellesley (1889–1956) was well known as a poet from the 1920s to the 1950s and published a number of collections. She married Lord Gerald Wellesley, later Seventh Duke of Wellington, in 1914; the couple had two children, but separated in 1923. She was a close friend of the poet and novelist Vita Sackville-West and was apparently one of her many lovers. She travelled very widely; with Vita Sackville-West she went to Persia and Russia, and she went several times to the East with Hilda Matheson, another of Vita's lovers. From 1928 she lived in Sussex in a house which she shared with Hilda Matheson.

Anna Wickham was the pen-name of Edith Harper, later Hepburn (1884–1947). Born at Wimbledon, brought up in Australia, she studied singing but gave it up to marry Patrick Hepburn, a lawyer, in 1906. They had four sons, one of whom died in infancy. Motherhood she enjoyed, but middle-class suburban married life did not suit her and became the subject of some biting satirical poetry; she and her husband separated in 1926. By this time Anna Wickham was in love with Natalie Barney, the expatriate American writer, with whom she corresponded for many years. She published several collections of her poems during her lifetime and more have appeared posthumously. A huge number remain in manuscript. She died by her own hand.

Wu Tsao lived in China in the first half of the nineteenth century. Born into a merchant family, she was married to a merchant, but her marriage was unhappy. She had many women lovers and wrote love poems to several courtesans. Her songs were very popular and were sung all over China. In about 1837 she withdrew to a secluded place and became a Taoist priestess.

PERMISSIONS

The editor is grateful for permission to include the following copyright material:

'We Press Buttons' from *R.A.W.* by Patience Agbabi (Gecko Press, 1995) is reprinted by permission of the author.

'Body Language' by Judith Barrington is reprinted by permission of the author. This poem first appeared in *Fireweed*, vol. 2, no. 3.

'Idyll' by Karin Boye, from *Complete Poems*, translated by David McDuff (Bloodaxe Books, 1994), reprinted courtesy of Bloodaxe Books.

'Four Beginnings/for Kyra' from *Beginning with O* by Olga Broumas (Yale University Press, 1977), reprinted by permission of Yale University Press. Copyright © 1977 by Olga Broumas.

'The Other' by Barbara Burford is reprinted by permission of the author. This poem was first published in *A Dangerous Knowing: Four Black Women Poets* (Sheba Feminist Publishers, 1985).

'Come slowly – Eden!' and 'I had been hungry, all the Years –': poems Nos. 211 and 579 by Emily Dickinson, reprinted by permission of the publishers and the Trustees of Amherst College from *The Poems of Emily Dickinson*, edited by Thomas H. Johnson, Cambridge, Mass.: The Belknap Press of Harvard University Press, copyright © 1951, 1955, 1979, 1983 by the President and Fellows of Harvard College.

'Words Without Echo' by Mary Dorcey, first published in *Kindling* (Onlywomen Press, 1982), reprinted in *Moving into the Spaces Cleared by Our Mothers* (Salmon Publishing, 1991). Reproduced by kind permission of the author.

'Close' is taken from *Mean Time* by Carol Ann Duffy, published by Anvil Press Poetry in 1993. Reprinted by permission.

'Preserves', 'You sleep now, my self in your arms' and 'The Garland: 16' from *Collected Poems 1949–1984* by Maureen Duffy (Hamish Hamilton, 1985), copyright © 1971, 1985 Maureen Duffy. Reprinted by permission of Jonathan Clowes Ltd on behalf of Maureen Duffy.

'White Wolf' by Christina Dunhill is reprinted by permission of the author. This poem first appeared in *Anvil New Poets 2*, edited by Carol Ann Duffy (Anvil Press Poetry, 1995).

'Going Under' by U. A. Fanthorpe, copyright U. A. Fanthorpe from *A Watching Brief* (1987), and '7301' by U. A. Fanthorpe, copyright U. A. Fanthorpe from *Neck Verse* (1992), both reproduced by permission of Peterloo Poets.

'Enclosures' is reprinted with permission from *Soft Engineering* by Kate Foley (Onlywomen Press Ltd, 1994).

'Song (October 1969)' by Kath Fraser is reprinted by permission of the author. This poem first appeared in *One Foot on the Mountain*, edited by Lilian Mohin (Onlywomen Press Ltd, 1979, 1980, 1982 and 1984).

'A Winter's Room' by Rhian Gallagher is reprinted by permission of the author. This poem first appeared in *The Rialto*, no. 30, Winter 1994.

'Region of No Birds' and 'Women at the Lakeside' reprinted from *Sapphic Songs: Eighteen to Eighty*, by Elsa Gidlow (Druid Heights, 1982), courtesy of Celeste West, Booklegger Publishing, Box 460654, San Francisco, CA 94146, USA.

'Love, you wicked dog' reprinted with permission from *The Work of a Common Woman* by Judy Grahn. © 1978. Published by The Crossing Press: Freedom, CA.

'Brown Girl' and 'A Mona Lisa' reprinted with permission from The Angelina Weld Grimké Papers, The Moorland-Spingarn Research Center, Howard University, Washington, DC, USA.

'White World' from *Collected Poems 1912–1944* by H.D. Copyright © 1982 by the estate of Hilda Doolittle. Reprinted from *Collected Poems 1912–1944*, edited by Louis L. Martz

(Carcanet, 1984), by permission of Carcanet Press Ltd.

'The Prophetical Songs' Nos. 2, 3, 8, 11 from *Sybil: The Glide of Her Tongue* by Gillian Hanscombe (Spinifex Press, 1992) is reprinted by permission of the author.

'In the Seventh Year' from *The Adoption Papers* by Jackie Kay (Bloodaxe Books, 1991) and 'Away from You' from *Other Lovers* by Jackie Kay (Bloodaxe Books, 1993), both reprinted courtesy of Bloodaxe Books.

'On a Night of the Full Moon', © 1992, 1973, 1970, 1968 by Audre Lorde, from *Undersong: Chosen Poems Old and New* by Audre Lorde. Reprinted with the approval of the Audre Lorde Estate.

'When My Love Lay Sleeping . . .' from *The Blue Donkey Fables* by Suniti Namjoshi (The Women's Press, 1988) is reprinted by permission of the author.

'In That Particular Temple' and 'We Can Compose Ourselves' from *Flesh and Paper* by Suniti Namjoshi and Gillian Hanscombe (Jezebel Tapes and Books, 1986) are reprinted by permission of the authors.

'Anna/Margaret' and 'Margaret/Anna' by Dorothy Nimmo are reprinted by permission of the author. These poems were published in *The North*, 20, and *The Children's Games* by Dorothy Nimmo (Smith/Doorstop Books, 1998).

'Restless Dialogue' from *The Dangerous World: New and Selected Poems, 1934–1994* by Naomi Replansky (Another Chicago Press, 1994) is reprinted by permission of the author.

Poem XIII of 'Twenty-One Love Poems', from *The Dream of a Common Language: Poems 1974–1977* by Adrienne Rich. Copyright © 1978 by W. W. Norton and Company, Inc. Reprinted by permission of the author and W. W. Norton and Company, Inc.

Poem 3 of 'Contradictions: Tracking Poems', from *Your Native Land, Your Life: Poems* by Adrienne Rich. Copyright © 1986 by Adrienne Rich. Reprinted by permission of the author and W. W. Norton and Company, Inc.

'The Transgress', by Muriel Rukeyser, from *The Collected Poems of Muriel Rukeyser*, 1978, McGraw-Hill, New York, by permission of William L. Rukeyser.

'Three Things' and 'Letters from Maine: 7' are from *Halfway to Silence* by May Sarton, first published by The Women's Press, 1993, and 'The Lady and the Unicorn' and 'On Being Given Time' are from *Coming Into Eighty and Earlier Poems* by May Sarton, first published by The Women's Press, 1995, and are used by permission of The Women's Press Ltd.

'Mouths', 'The Heron' and 'There are never enough love poems' by Jan Sellers are reprinted by permission of the author. 'Mouths' was published in *New Prospect Poetry*, Spring 1990. 'The Heron' was published in *Critical Quarterly*, vol. 36, no. 2, Summer 1994.

'The Passion of Remembrance' by Dorothea Smartt is reprinted by permission of the author. This poem first appeared in *An Intimate Wilderness: Lesbian Writers on Sexuality*, edited by Judith Barrington (Eighth Mountain Press, 1991).

'Private Love' and 'When the Lights Go Up' by Cherry Smyth are reprinted by permission of the author. 'Private Love' was published in *Virago New Poets*, edited by Melanie Silgardo and Janet Beck (Virago Press, 1993). 'When the Lights Go Up' was published in *As Girls Could Boast: New Poetry by Women*, edited by Christina Dunhill (Oscars Press, 1994).

'Riddle Game' by Gillian Spraggs was published in *Whatever You Desire: A Book of Lesbian Poetry*, edited by Mary Jo Bang (Oscars Press, 1990) and is the author's copyright.

'Equilibrist' from *The Love Poems of May Swenson*. Copyright © 1991 by The Literary Estate of May Swenson. Reprinted by permission of Houghton Mifflin Company. All rights reserved.

'Drawing you, heavy with sleep' and 'In April' are reprinted from *Collected Poems of Sylvia Townsend Warner*, edited by Claire Harman (Carcanet New Press, 1982) by permission of Carcanet Press Ltd.

'Song' ('Your spirit is my treasury') and 'The Hare' by Anna Wickham reprinted by permission of the Estate of Anna Wickham. Permission to use the line 'Love, love, the dogs are after me' from 'The Hare' as the epigraph to a section of poems given by the Estate of Anna Wickham.

'For the Courtesan Ch'ing Lin' and 'Bitter rain in my courtyard' by Wu Tsao, translated by Kenneth Rexroth and Ling Chung, from *The Orchid Boat: Women Poets of China*. Copyright © 1973 by Kenneth Rexroth and Ling Chung. Reprinted by permission of New Directions Publishing Corp.

The editor is grateful to Professor Peter Dronke for his permission to publish her translation of the Latin verse-letter 'G. unice sue rose'. The original text may be found in *Medieval Latin and the Rise of European Love-Lyric* by Peter Dronke (Clarendon Press, Oxford; 2nd edition, 1968), vol. II, pp. 480–81.

All translations from Sappho, Nossis, Erinna, Bieiris de Romans, Sor Juana Inés de la Cruz and Renée Vivien are by the editor and are her copyright. Three of the translations from Sappho were published in 'Divine Visitations: Sappho's Poetry of Love' by Gillian Spraggs, in *What Lesbians Do in Books*, edited by Elaine Hobby and Chris White (The Women's Press, 1991). The translation of Fragment 31 ('He seems to me the peer of gods, that man') has been slightly altered. The translation of Erinna's *The Spindle: Lament for Baucis* previously appeared in *Man Does, Woman Is: An Anthology of Work and Gender*, edited by Marion Shaw (Faber and Faber, 1995)

Every effort has been made to trace the original copyright holders, but in at least one instance this has not been possible. It is hoped any such omission from this list will be excused.

INDEX OF POETS

INDEX OF TITLES AND FIRST LINES